Fantastic Flowerpots

50 Creative Ways to Decorate a Plain Pot

Bobbe Needham

Lark Books

Asheville, North Carolina

Editor: Bobbe Needham
Design and art direction: Celia Naranjo
Photography: Evan Bracken
Production: Celia Naranjo
Editorial assistance: Heather Smith
Proofreader: Jackieann Wilson
Library of Congress Cataloging-in-Publication Data Available

10 9 8 7 6 5 4 3 2

Published by Lark Books
50 College St.
Asheville, NC 28801, USA

© 1998, Lark Books

For information about distribution in the U.S., Canada, the U.K., Europe, and Asia, call Lark Books at 828-253-0467.

Distributed in Australia by Capricorn Link (Australia) Pty Ltd., P.O. Box 6651, Baulkham Hills Business Centre, NSW 2153, Australia

Distributed in New Zealand by Southern Publishers Group, 22 Burleigh St., Grafton, Auckland, NZ

Printed in Hong Kong

ISBN 1-57990-143-3

CREDITS AND KUDOS

Kudos, with gratitude, to all the imaginative and cooperative designers who contributed pots to this book...to designer and production artist Celia Naranjo for her wonderful artistic eye and especially for a gorgeous cover, twice...to photographer Evan Bracken of Light Reflections, the calmest gun in the West...to Deborah Morgenthal for nick-of-time advice and help...and to Heather Smith, competent and creative editorial assistant, for Internet and library research, countless phone calls, and the dirt dessert.

For photographic props, thanks to Natural Home, Asheville, North Carolina, to Dana Irwin and Rosemary Kast of Lark Books, and to Jan Cope and Maya Contento, plant-growing friends.

Thanks for interviews and photographs to Ward Ritter of F.W. Ritter Sons & Co. (pages 22 and 23) and Walter Potenza, chef-owner of La Locanda del Coccio (the Inn of Clay) in Providence, Rhode Island (page 51). The photographs of the terra-cotta army on pages 10 and 105, from *The Terra Cotta Army of Emperor Quin* by Caroline Lazo, published by MacMillan, are used with the kind permission of photographer Dr. Robert Jacobsen.

Other photo credits: page 33, Mijn Tuin, Haarlem; Netherlands; page 8, Ariadne, Haarlem, Netherlands; page 63.

Contents

Introduction

This book has a kind of split personality. On one hand, since it's about decorating flowerpots, it needs to devote some space to plants and container gardening. On the other hand, its about decorating *terra-cotta* flowerpots, and terra-cotta turns out to be an interesting subject in itself.

I just wanted to prepare you.

OF POTS AND PLANTS

Judging from the numbers and varieties of plant pots on display at even the smallest nursery, florist, or feed-and-seed (not to mention the armies of pots arrayed at big garden centers), we are obsessed with plants, pots, gardening, or all three. Now that so few of us live on farms, now that vast numbers of us have no access to soil that goes deeper than our patio planters or our apartment window boxes, we've evidently become container-garden maniacs.

And lots of us do our container gardening in some form of terra-cotta pot. Although most of the pots in this book were chosen for their common-garden-variety character, a grand choice of shapes and sizes faces us when we go pots shopping. Some pots are highly specialized, like strawberry pots (see page 76), orchid pots (page 69), or "Long Toms" for plants with long roots (pages 54 and 55). You can find special pots for growing bulbs, crocuses, seedlings—all of which do fine in more ordinary pots, as long as they're planted right.

And why wouldn't we love container gardening, or at least appreciate the people who do? What living space wouldn't benefit from a bright group of flowering plants—big bronze chrysanthemums, yellow daisies, creamy lilies? Or a row of friendly, fragrant herbs on a kitchen window sill? Or a holiday arrangement of Christmas cactus, poinsettias, and miniature hollies? Don't we covet those patios and little cement decks bursting with green life and splashes of flowery color, geraniums and impatiens and all those other blooms we don't know the names of? Don't we appreciate watching paper-white narcissus bloom in a pot in the middle of winter, and early crocuses indoors in February?

Even if we love flowers and plants, many of us balk at...actually gardening. Doing the work. Remembering to water—or, more often, not to water. Putting ourselves through the grief of losing one plant after another.

One of the messages of this book is this: You can enjoy decorating flowerpots without ever touching a living plant. You can give the pots away...you can use them for something other than plants...you can make someone else put plants in them and take care of them.

On the other hand, you might be ready to try again...or to venture out for the first time into the bush leagues of container gardening. You may have changed...your living space may have changed...the plants available have certainly changed...and now you'll have some fantastic flowerpots to put them in.

On Terra-Cotta

Terra-cotta, which translates literally from the Italian as "cooked earth," is a hard-baked, usually reddish brown clay that various cultures have for more than 5,500 years turned into pottery, sculpture, and architectural decoration—in fact entire buildings (the famous Harrod's store in South Kensington, London, is sheathed in tawny terra-cotta).

Terra-cotta's characteristic color comes from iron oxide in the clay, which turns red when fired.

As lovely and fragile as terra-cotta pots are, terra-cotta itself, when used for example for architectural decoration, properly

maintained has greater staying power than stone. (Don't let your pots winter outdoors, though—alternating freezes and thaws will shatter them.)

If you cared to think about it, you could probably figure out what people first used terra-cotta pots for—cooking and storing food. In fact, cooking in terra-cotta, which has remained popular in Italy, is a recent innovation in fine U.S. restaurants (see page 51).

The best-known terra-cotta sculptors have been Italian—Donatello and the Della Robbias, uncle Luca and nephew Andrea. But no terra-cotta sculptures have fired the modern imagination like the recent discovery of a life-sized terra-cotta army buried 2,200 years ago near Beijing, China, whose first warriors were unearthed in 1974 (see photo).

Gardeners discovered the advantages of terra-cotta as early as Ancient Roman times. Since then, throughout the world, terra-cotta pots have graced growing spaces of all kinds, from formal French and Italian gardens to cozy British flats and Caribbean cottages, from Asian temple grounds to terraces in Texas and patios in Pennsylvania.

About the Projects

Each *Fantastic Flowerpots* project starts with a common terra-cotta pot you can pick up at any garden center. Just two reminders. First, a 6" (15cm) pot is 6" (15cm) in diameter *across the top*, an 8" (21cm) pot 8" (21cm) in diameter, and so on. Second, any pot that may get wet, such as one that

will hold a live plant, needs to be sealed with polyurethane before and after you decorate it (don't neglect the bottom or the drainage hole); at that point, the

terra-cotta is no longer porous. The pot takes on the characteristics of a plastic pot, that is, if you put plants in it, they will need less water.

You may decide to use many of the pots you decorate as *pot containers*, setting another pot inside them—in that case, you don't need to worry about waterproofing.

Most of what you need to know to create the projects in this book you learned in kindergarten: painting for fun, gluing, cutting with scissors, stamping, sponging. You can reproduce a project, or use one as a place to start—an idea, a motif, a technique that provides a springboard for your own pot decorating.

The instructions with each project tell you what size pot the designer used (if that's important to the design), what materials, how many coats of paint, and so

on, but your own experiments are sure to lead you to your own discoveries. Among the comforting things about decorating pots is their low cost (and the low cost of decorating materials), and the range of solutions for cracked or otherwise apparently imperfect pots (see page 103).

May your pot-decorating creativity flourish and grow, along with your small terra-cotta gardens!

(see page 103).

Before You Begin

Any terra-cotta pot that may get wet—including one that will hold a live plant—needs to be sprayed or painted with a protective polyurethane coating before and after you decorate it. Be sure the sealant reaches every bit of terra-cotta, including the bottom and the drainage hole—otherwise the clay will absorb moisture and your paint may bubble or crack. Since the need for sealing depends on a pot's ultimate use, some designers sealed their pots, some didn't—so not all instructions call for this step. To be certain to avoid heartbreak, seal every pot.

Just Paint

Ancient World

Designer: Katherine Graham

The old-world look of these pots, with their Phoenician boats and North African figures and symbols, is only enhanced by the "aging" of hard-water mineral deposits. With no preparation and requiring only a marking pen, these are the "simplest" pots in the book.

Materials

New, clean terra-cotta pots
Black indelible marker (laundry marker) or
brush, pen, pen nibs, India ink

What to Do

Paint your designs straight onto the pots—no preparation required. Both laundry marker and India ink are indelible. The pot stays porous, and the ink stays on it. Katherine Graham's designs were inspired by books on ancient-world art.

Color Washes

Designer: Nancy McGaha

With this color-wash technique you can produce all kinds of effects, depending on the colors you choose, how you group them, where you place the pots, and of course what you put in them. A quick and easy way to put color right where you want it.

Materials

5" (13cm) terra-cotta pots

Paintbrush

Water

Latex paint in your chosen colors

What to Do

Oh, so simple. Start with clean pots. With a brush slightly dampened in water, brush a little paint on the pot, and continue stroking until you get the effect you want. As the paint dries you can stroke off excess paint. Texture and depth of color vary based on the ratio of water to paint on your brush—more water for a more washed look. Vary the appearance of some pots by blending colors, if you like.

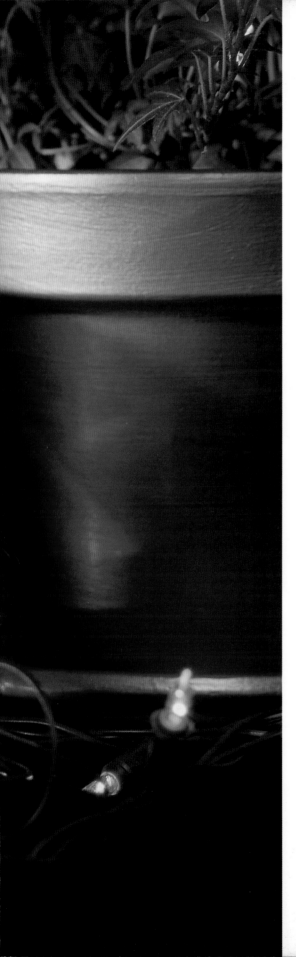

 # Precious Metals

DESIGNERS: ELENA LANGE AND NANCY McGAHA

These glowing pots add special glitter to holidays, but they're also just right for the showiest of flowering plants all through the year. And they're striking in a group of three or more—the perfect settings for precious plants.

MATERIALS

Terra-cotta pots and saucers

¾" or ⅝" (2cm) acrylic paintbrush

8 oz. (240ml) of water-base sealer,
matte finish

Metallic spray paint in gold, aluminum,
and/or copper

12 oz. (360ml) of clear acrylic spray, gloss
finish

Candles (optional)

WHAT TO DO

So simple! Seal the pots and saucers inside and out by brushing on two coats of sealer, then two coats of your chosen metallic spray paint, then a coat of acrylic spray finish. The only thing to remember: always allow one coat to dry before you apply the next.

POT SHOT

Add zest, color, and panache to your cuisine with edible flowers. For a peppery flavor in salads, try sprinkling nasturtiums over your tossed greens. Other decorative and tasty flowers are borage, chives, roses, and pansies. Snip off the flower heads just at serving time so they're fresh.

Pots and Candles

- **Safety warning:** If you plan to put a candle in a terra-cotta pot, be sure to seal the pot's inside with two coats of water-base sealer. Otherwise, because the unsealed clay is porous, it can act as a large wick.
- The easiest pot-and-candle combination is to place already-made candles in the pots, as in the photo. They're easily replaced, and you can vary color and scent as you please. You'll probably want to plug the pot hole with caulking putty or silicone.
- If you choose to pour a candle into your pot, follow the same safety precautions, then treat the pot as you would any other container for candles.

Plain Geometry

Designer: Pamella Wilson

Simplicity usually is all it's cracked up to be, and a grouping of striped and checked pots can be more charming (and far easier to produce) than the most "arty" creation. You can try circles, triangles, rectangles—but plain stripes and checks are hard to beat for high-style geometrics.

Materials

Terra-cotta pots

Acrylic paints (here, red, black, and white)

Paintbrushes

Pencil

Masking tape

What To Do

Tape your design on the pot, then trace the tape with pencil and remove the tape. For striped pots, of course, you can paint the stripes with the masking tape still on.

Where Terra-Cotta Pots Come From

The terra-cotta pots you buy in Ft. Myers, Florida, or Terre Haute, Indiana, are as likely to have traveled from factories in Germany, China, Brazil, or Mexico as from a U.S. manufactory. "Only three pot manufacturers are left in the United States," says Ward Ritter, whose F.W. Ritter Sons & Co. in South Rockwood, Michigan, is one of them. "There used to be twenty. They folded because of the imports," which can be made and shipped for considerably less than U.S. costs.

F.W. Ritter Sons turns out 135,000 to 150,000 terra-cotta pots a day. Like many manufacturers, they mine their own clay on site—that yellow glacial clay is what drew them to their Michigan location.

It turns out that such factories simply use a large-scale version of the familiar raw-clay-to-kiln process. They strip-mine the clay, then work out the impurities with a filter press system. At this point the clay "looks like a big pancake," Ritter says. Then they grind it back up with a chopper and the clay is extruded in a pug mill to remove air that would cause it to crack or break when fired. It's extruded once more and pressed into molds, dried, and fired in kilns.

How many pots at a time? "One," Ritter says, "but 4,000 to 8,000 in an eight-hour shift."

Although F.W. Ritter Sons is the same "small family business" it's been since its founding in 1893, it is also one of the world's leading manufacturers of clay flowerpots, and a classic American success story. Ward Ritter and his brother, Fred, are fourth-generation owners. Fred Ritter, Sr., a German immigrant in the late 1800s, began by making and selling small glazed-clay objects at country fairs, moved on to clay

Ritter pots still wet from the molds, on their way to the dryer.

A variety of pots after firing—or "burning"—at the Ritter factory.

flowerpots for local growers, and in 1921 bought the clay-rich Michigan farm where the company flourishes today.

Or flourishes on most days. "I have three sons and my brother has a son," Ward Ritter says. "We're hoping to pass it on to them, if the imports don't get too strong. But they may not want the headaches."

Warehoused pots ready for shipping. Over half of Ritter's 75 employees work in shipping, the rest in production.

Black-on-White Birds

DESIGNER: JEAN WALL PENLAND

This pot calls for an ancient and sophisticated artist's technique called "drawing with a squeeze bottle." For some mysterious reason, it's easier and more fun than painting with a brush and works especially well for simple figures and geometric designs (that is, more the stick-figure than the Rembrandt school).

MATERIALS

Terra-cotta pot
White acrylic paint
Paintbrush
Thick black acrylic paint or black gesso
Squeeze bottle

WHAT TO DO

1. Paint the pot with the white acrylic paint.
2. Fill the squeeze bottle with the acrylic paint or gesso, and draw your favorite images on the pot.

DESIGNER'S TIP

❋ Your design is strengthened by repetition, even when this repetition is somewhat varied, as in the group of disparate but "familial" birds on the pot shown here.

Herbs

DESIGNER: MAYA CONTENTO

Everyone's life can benefit from a few fragrant herbs growing on a windowsill. Here, Latin names for thyme, rosemary, and chives, with their initial letters "illuminated" as tiny herb gardens, add a classical and classy touch.

MATERIALS

Clean terra cotta pot and saucer

Masking tape

Acrylic paint

Paintbrush and paint pen

Clear, waterproof acrylic sealant

Herb book with illustrations,
live plants or stencils

WHAT TO DO

1. Apply a base coat of acrylic paint to the pot and saucer. Let dry.
2. Select the herb you want to use and plan the design for the herb name and drawing on the pot.
3. With a brush or paint pen, paint the pattern for the herb-garden detail, then fill in the rest of the herb name.
4. Paint or stencil an image of each herb alongside its name.
5. Decorate the edges of the pot and saucer.
6. When the paint is dry, coat with waterproof acrylic sealer.

# Mountains of the Moon

DESIGNER: JAN COPE

Evocative pots whose apparent simplicity for once is not mis-leading—they really are easy to paint, whether you live in sight of mountains or not.

POT SHOT

Most plant people swear by terra-cotta (clay) pots...or by plastic pots.

Clay pots are

- heavy, so less liable to tip over.
- porous, so plants are less likely to get water-logged and damaging salts are leached away from the potting mix.
- more aesthetically pleasing than plastic, to many people, partly because they're made of a natural material.

Plastic pots are

- lightweight, so large pots are easier to move around.
- nonporous, so less watering is needed.
- almost unbreakable, even if you drop them.
- easy to clean.
- colorful and inexpensive.

Pot choice seems to be, like so many other of life's little decisions, mainly subjective.

MATERIALS

Terra-cotta pot and saucer
Acrylic paints in your choice of colors
Small paintbrushes
Pencil
Urethane sealer and large paintbrush
Water

WHAT TO DO

1. Paint the entire pot and saucer with a thin coat of urethane sealer and let dry overnight.
2. If you like, draw your design on the pot in pencil. Paint on one color at a time and let dry, following the design in the photograph...adding your own embellishments. Decorate the saucer.
3. When the pot and saucer are complete and dry, seal both with another thin coat of urethane.

All You Really Need to Know (to Keep Your Plants Alive)

🌺 **Don't drown them.** We beginners hear this, but we don't believe it. Keeping the potting mix wet all the time will kill most plants. Most (but not all) flowering plants need watering whenever the soil surface is dry. Most (but not all) foliage house plants need watering thoroughly and often from spring to autumn, but in winter need to let the top ½ inch of soil dry out between waterings. Cacti and succulents need frequent watering from spring to autumn, but in winter the soil should be allowed to dry out almost completely. Every species is different. Don't guess about watering.

🌺 **Let them rest.** One of the reasons for winter is so that plants can rest, indoors or out. Nearly all plants need less water, less heat, and less feeding then.

🌺 **Be a good realtor.** The top three real estate rules apply to plants' homes as well as people's: location, location, location. No one can make an aspidistra thrive in a sunny window, or grow happy cacti in a dimly lit hallway.

🌺 **Raise the humidity, especially in winter.** Plants need moist air. In a room with central heating, you can group pots together, mist the foliage (spray all sides of the leaves with tepid water, in the morning), or double pot (put the pot in an outer waterproof container and fill the space between with moist peat).

🌺 **Learn to repot.** Often the only problem with unhappy plants is that they've outgrown their pots. (You can tell if they barely grow even in spring and summer, if the soil dries out fast, or if roots are growing out the drainage hole. When you take them out of the pot, you'll see a matted mass of roots around the soil.) Repotting into a slightly larger pot, preferably in the spring, is the solution.

Mexican

DESIGNER: LIZ HUGHEY

In this feel-good pot, bright colors and simple designs complement the already warm tone of terra-cotta to evoke south-of-the-border sunshine and fiestas. It's the perfect home for multihued crotons like the Bush-on-Fire variety pictured here (a native of Sri Lanka).

MATERIALS

Terra-cotta pot

Masking tape

Acrylic paint in the colors of your choice

Paintbrushes

Black paint pen

WHAT TO DO

1. Lay out the stripes around the pot with strips of masking tape (a challenge because of the sloping pot sides)—these areas will remain the original terra-cotta shade. Vary the width of the strips and stripes as you please. The tape needs to adhere tight to the pot so that paint can't slip in under its edges.

2. Paint the spaces between the tape with the colors of your choice, and let the paint dry completely.

3. Pull off the tape and paint figures and designs on the stripes with the paint pen.

Combed Lattices

DESIGNER: ELENA LANGE

These handsome pots look terrific with any variety of plant, from all foliage to elegant lilies to many-flowered plants like cyclamen or begonias. Even cactus. They're produced with a simplified sgraffito technique—scratching through one layer of paint to reveal another.

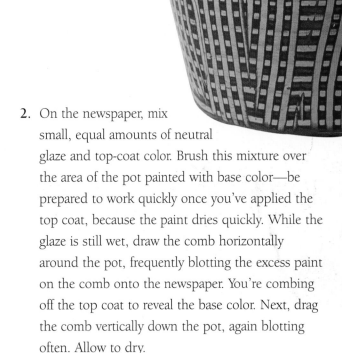

MATERIALS

6" terra-cotta pots and saucers

Small acrylic paintbrush—¾" or ⅝" (2cm) #10 works well

Multipurpose craft comb (or cardboard equivalent)

8 oz. (240ml) of water-base sealer, matte finish

2 oz. (60ml) of neutral glaze

2 oz. (60ml) of acrylic paint in your colors of choice. For the pots pictured:

For the green:
robin's-egg blue (base) and emerald

For the blue:
baby blue (base) and medium blue

For the maroon:
light rose (base) and burgundy

Newspaper

Clear acrylic spray, gloss finish

WHAT TO DO

1. Apply two coats of sealer to the entire pot and saucer, then two to four coats of the base color to the outside of the pots up to the rim and to the lower outside base of the saucer. (Dark colors may need only two coats, lighter colors three or four.) *Be sure each coat of sealer and paint is dry before you apply the next.*

2. On the newspaper, mix small, equal amounts of neutral glaze and top-coat color. Brush this mixture over the area of the pot painted with base color—be prepared to work quickly once you've applied the top coat, because the paint dries quickly. While the glaze is still wet, draw the comb horizontally around the pot, frequently blotting the excess paint on the comb onto the newspaper. You're combing off the top coat to reveal the base color. Next, drag the comb vertically down the pot, again blotting often. Allow to dry.

3. Apply two to four coats of the top-coat color to the pot rim, outside and inside, and to the upper exterior rim and entire inside of the saucer. Allow to dry between coats.

4. Spray the finished pots and saucers with two coats of acrylic finish, allowing them to dry between coats.

Christmas Balls

DESIGNER: PAMELLA WILSON

Festive, fun, and freehand—If you can draw lines and circles, here's a simple, bright pot to plant with Christmas cactus, poinsettias, holly—or matching Christmas-tree balls—for a bloomin' miracle of a seasonal gift.

MATERIALS

Terra-cotta pot
Acrylic paint: white, blue, green, yellow, red, pink
Small and medium paintbrushes
Pencil
Polyurethane spray sealant

WHAT TO DO

1. Paint the pot (inside and out, or just the outside) with a coat of white acrylic paint and let dry.

2. Sketch in your Christmas-tree balls or other design with pencil—as many Christmas-tree balls on the pot as meets your need for festiveness. Paint the balls, allowing each color to dry before painting the next.

3. When the design is completely dry, spray the entire pot, inside and out, with two coats of polyurethane sealant, allowing it to dry between coats.

Flowerpots for Friends: Special Gift-Giving Ideas

❀ Create a pot-et-fleur, called that because it sounds much fancier in French than in English: "pot and flower." The easiest method is to plant a large pot with a variety of foliage house plants, and in the center to "plant" a florist tube or small narrow jar. When you're ready to present the gift, fill the tube with water and arrange seasonal cut flowers in it—daffodils in spring, roses in summer, holly at Christmas.

❀ For some welcome winter cheer, buy an assortment of bulbs from late summer onwards or budding bulbs in late fall. Try iris, snowdrops, grape hyacinths, and the old standbys—hyacinths, narcissi, and crocuses. In one of your own hand-decorated pots, plant the bulbs close together so they provide support for each other and fill the gaps with potting material. Cover with a thick mulch of moss to hold in the moisture. Your friend will need to place the pot in a bright spot away from direct heat and keep the soil and moss moist. (For more on bulbs, see pages 96–97.)

Roll up small hand towels and arrange them in a pamper-yourself pot for the bath—a loofah sponge, bubble bath, aromatic soap, body wash, foam squeegie, after-bath splash, rubber ducky.

❀ Arrange kitchen towels so that their edges drape like leaves over the top of a colorful pot. Fill the pot with wooden spoons, a wire whisk, pot holders, a garlic press, a *good* vegetable peeler...whatever you covet in those snazzy chef's boutiques—and top it off with a string of garlic or bright peppers.

❀ Take a "living pot" to a soiree for a knock-'em-dead centerpiece—cover a pot with live leaves and fill with a sumptuous arrangement of seasonal cut flowers or a flowering plant. (See page 100–101.)

❀ Welcome a new baby with something besides pastel. Decoupage a pot with the front page—and maybe the comics—from the baby's birth day—aged for a slightly antique look. Plant it with a bright flowering plant or make it a pot-et-fleur.

❀ Give an enthusiastic cook two or three decorated pots planted with fresh herbs, or a handsome windowbox of potted herbs (see page 82).

Give a gift that combines color and scent, one of the miniature citrus trees available at nurseries. The fragrant blossoms of Citrus mitis, a dwarf orange that grows up to three feet (1m) tall, give way to tiny bright fruit, too inedible for anything but marmalade. Decorate an especially citrus-appropriate pot (limes, oranges, and yellows) or present it in an "aged" pot, to evoke sunny Mediterranean groves.

Pansies, Roses, and Daisies

Designer: Maya Contento

These pots present a delightful echo of the flowers blooming in them—although no flowerpot police will arrest you for planting violets in your roses pot. Even if you decide to use stencils for the flowers, you might care to try some freehand leaves, stems, and buds.

Materials

Clean terra-cotta pot and saucer

Masking tape

Acrylic paint in two contrasting bright colors

Paintbrush

Clear acrylic sealant

Flower and leaf stencils (optional)

What to Do

1. Mask the rim of the pot with tape.
2. Coat the body of the pot with a bright shade of acrylic paint and let dry.
3. Remove the tape and use a fresh strip around the pot just below the rim.
4. Paint the rim and saucer in a contrasting color and let dry
5. Paint a simple, repeating flower pattern with leaves (either freehand or with stencils) around the body of the pot and let dry.
6. Apply a coat of clear acrylic sealant.

Polka Dots

DESIGNER: PAMELLA WILSON

Cheerful, charming pots that lend themselves to endless color variations, reminiscent of dotted-swiss curtains blowing over sunny windows...or freckles.

MATERIALS

Terra-cotta pot
Enamel spray paint: white plus blue, green, or colors you choose
Orange acrylic paint
Small paintbrush

WHAT TO DO

1. Lightly spray the outside of the pot with alternating coats of white and a second color of your choice. Add a fifth coat of white to produce a lighter shade. Let dry after each coat.
2. With a small paintbrush, add orange polka dots, as in the photograph.

EASY-CARE PLANTS FOR YOUR POTS

If you consider yourself a "black thumb" kind of gardener, that is, if your house plants consistently die before their time or if no one ever asks you to take care of their plants, even people who trust you with their children...there's still hope.

These plant groups are practically indestructible: sansevieria (mother-in-law's tongue and snake plant), fatsia (Japanese aralia and castor-oil plant), and aspidistra (cast-iron plant). Umbrella plants, if you keep them wet. Most succulents, if you keep them dry, especially in winter.

The secret to survival for your umbrella plants is to keep the roots always wet. Put the pot in a saucer or tray, and keep water in that outer container. Pick a dwarf variety if you have limited space, and plan to repot every spring.

Among the succulents (plants with fleshy leaves and stems that store water)—consider a selection of cacti. Small ones that flower might make you feel better. Or try a cobweb houseleek—they thrive on neglect and give you red flowers in summer. Sedums are unusual looking and offer visual variety—look for types called jelly beans, Christmas cheer, and donkey's tail. The aloes are also forgiving (and are great for kitchens, for their juice is a natural burn ointment). Also quite safe are members of the tradescantia group: the fast-growing inch plants or the fur-covered teddy bear vine.

The secrets to not killing succulents are: put them on a windowsill so they'll get plenty of light; in summer, give them fresh air and water normally (when the soil gets dry); water only about once every six weeks in winter; repot only when you must—when they're bursting out of their pot.

Other plants you might trust yourself with include spider plants—a familiar hanging plant with variegated leaves—and climbing ivies like grape ivy or common ivy.

Everyone deserves to have plants if they want them. It's mostly a matter of memory: remembering you have them.

Hard-to-kill plants for your pots include, from left to right, jade plant, common ivy, and aloe. Jade and aloe are both succulents.

Faux Finish
and
Decoupage

# Divine Decoupage

DESIGNER: JEAN TOMASO MOORE

Decoupage knows no bounds or limits. Almost any paper works—add some decoupage glue and paint, and you have an original pot custom made for any room, decor, mood—or friend.

MATERIALS

8" (21cm) terra-cotta pots

Decorative paper prints

Decoupage medium

Paintbrush or sponge brush

Sponge

Cuticle scissors

Craft knife

Acrylic craft paints or spray paints: one dark color, one light color, to complement the prints

Waxed paper

Water

Spray acrylic sealer

Note: You'll find decoupage medium at a craft store.

WHAT TO DO

1. Brush on a thick coat of decoupage medium to seal the outside of the pot, and let it dry. Brush on the lighter color of acrylic paint as a base coat on the entire outside of the pot, and let it dry.

2. With the darker acrylic paint, either sponge or spray paint. To sponge: Dampen the sponge with water, squeeze out the excess, and lightly dab the paint on the pot until you are happy with the amount of coverage. Or, to spray: Spray on one or two coats of paint.

3. When the paint is dry, apply another thin layer of decoupage medium and allow it to dry.

4. To cut out your paper design, cut away interior areas first with the craft knife. Cut out the rest with cuticle scissors, angling the curve of the scissors away from the print.

5. Check the positioning of the print against the pot for best placement.

6. Lay the cut-out print right side down on waxed paper and brush a thin coat of decoupage medium on the back. Gently place the print on the pot, smoothing the paper as you go. Press it onto the pot with a slightly dampened sponge, working small sections at a time to work out the bubbles and creases. Allow to dry thoroughly.

7. Brush four or five coats of decoupage medium over the entire surface, allowing it to dry between coats. Finish by spraying with a coat of acrylic sealer.

❈ DESIGNER'S TIPS ❈

❈ Any decorative paper works for decoupage—calendars, cards, magazines, canned-food labels, garden catalogs, postage stamps. I cut the sun, moon, stars, cabbage roses, and butterflies from gift wrap. I photocopied the green peas and hand colored them with pencils.

❈ Bigger designs without intricate and delicate parts are easiest to cut out.

Malachite and Coral Marbles

DESIGNER: SHARON TOMPKINS

Whether their lustrous swirls remind you of Italian marble or semiprecious stones, these glowing pots are riches in themselves or luscious settings for emerald-leaved plants.

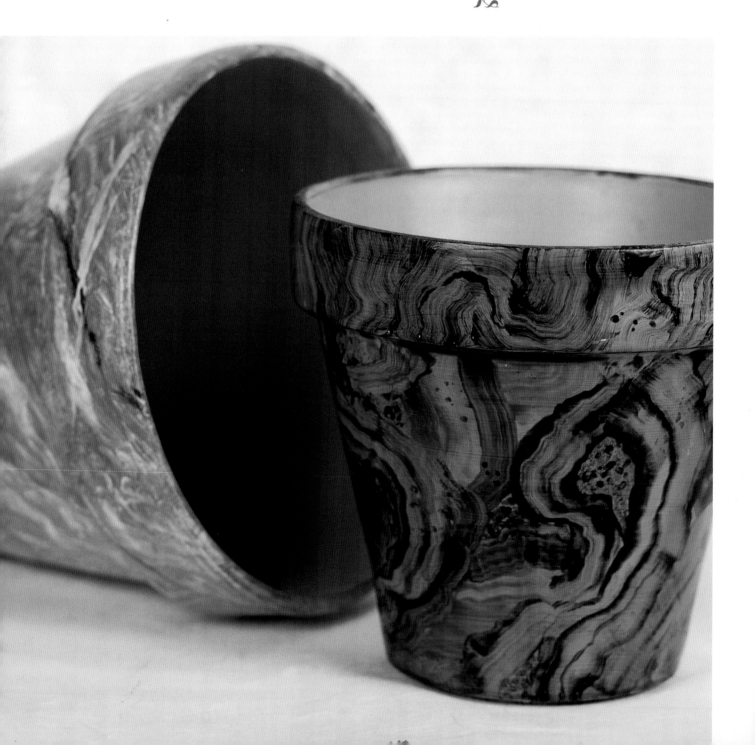

MATERIALS

For the malachite pot

Terra-cotta pot

Water-base glazing liquid

Satin varnish spray

1" (2.5cm) latex or artist's brush

Thin cardboard

Small artist's brush

Base coat and interior: pale teal latex or craft
acrylic paint

Glaze: dark green latex or acrylic paint

For the coral pot, substitute:

Base coat: off-white latex paint

Glazes: burgundy, dark rust, gold, brown,
and black latex paints

Interior: medium blue latex paint

*Note: Directions are for the malachite pot. For the coral
pot, substitute the paint colors listed.*

WHAT TO DO

1. Paint the pot inside and out, with the 1"
   (2.5cm) brush and two base coats of teal,
   allowing each coat to dry.
2. Mix dark green paint, glazing liquid, and water
   in a 4:4:2 ratio. (Here, use 2 oz. each of paint
   and glazing liquid and 1 oz. of water, or 60ml,
   60ml, and 30ml.) Paint the mixture on about
   one-third of the pot, from top to bottom.
3. Tear off a piece of cardboard 1" to 2" (2.5 to
   5cm) by about ½" (1.5cm). Drag it through the
   wet glaze in curves and circles, jiggling it as
   you go.
4. Repeat steps 2 and 3 with another third of the
   pot, then with the final third.

5. Add some darker accents, using the glaze-latex
   mixture and the artist's brush to spatter, dab,
   or streak within the broad bands of color.
   Allow the pot to dry.
6. Spray the pot with two coats of varnish, allowing it to dry after each coat.
7. Paint the inside of the pot with a contrasting
   color or a final coat of the base coat.

Georgia O'Keeffe Stamps

DESIGNER: JEAN WALL PENLAND

You don't have to be a fan of either O'Keeffe or the U.S. Postal Service to appreciate this striking pot, just an aficionado of great color combinations. The number of variations on this design seems limited only by the number and locations of your pen pals.

MATERIALS

Terra-cotta pot and saucer

Black acrylic paint

Paintbrush

Stamps

Glue stick

Gold acrylic paint

Small flat brush, ⅛" (.5cm) wide

Image of Georgia O'Keeffe, or other
appropriate image

Matte varnish

WHAT TO DO

1. Paint the inside and outside of the pot with black acrylic paint. If you need a second coat, let dry between coats.
2. Use a glue stick to glue the stamps in columns around the pot.
3. With a small flat brush, paint the margins between the stamps with gold acrylic paint. You may need up to four coats.
4. Glue the image of Georgia O'Keeffe (or the image of your choice) onto the gold area.
5. Apply two coats of matte varnish to protect the finish and stamps, allowing the varnish to dry between coats.

DESIGNER'S TIPS

❀ You can always purchase new stamps from the post office, but if you feel more adventurous, get used stamps at flea markets or stamp-collecting exchanges—philatelic bourses. Most collectors at an exchange don't want used stamps, so you can often find boxes full for pennies apiece.

❀ You can paint the terra-cotta saucer either black or a rich orange-red to match the Georgia O'Keeffe poppies on the stamps, or a color that complements the stamps you choose.

Hobbit Cottage

DESIGNER: CATHY SMITH

A delightful pot to see you through a cold winter into spring—and you can take your time painting it on those long winter evenings, letting its charm warm you as you go. You can follow the quite detailed instructions, or take off on your own cottage-designing spree. 🪶

MATERIALS

8" (20cm) terra-cotta pot

Gloss acrylic varnish or decoupage medium

Gloss oil-base polyurethane

Acrylic craft paint: light cream, deep salmon, charcoal grey, dark green, mustard, turquoise, apple green, medium green, dark blue grey, and medium brown

Red or brown charcoal pencil

Vinyl eraser

Permanent fine-point black marker

Acrylic crackle medium

White craft glue

Paper for name scroll and sconces

Paintbrushes: #1 or #2, #4 round, and #14 round

Water

Plate or pie tin for a palette

Small, flexible sea sponge

Round-ended toothpick

Note: You'll find crackle medium and decoupage medium at craft stores.

WHAT TO DO

1. Paint the entire pot with two coats of dark green acrylic, with #14 brush, allowing it to dry between coats.

2. Paint crackle medium on the entire outside of the pot below the rim, following the directions on the label for application and drying time.

3. *When you paint over crackle medium, be sure to have enough paint on your brush to make a full uninterrupted stroke. Don't go back over a stroke to correct coverage. The finish should look irregular and antique.* With #14 brush, use vertical strokes to apply turquoise paint over the crackle medium. Allow to dry overnight.

4. Following the photo, with charcoal pencil, draw in the two doors, windows, trim, planter, stone decks, and woodpile. Fill in with charcoal grey paint and let dry.

5. Now sketch in details—planks in the door, stonework, window pane, logs, etc. With #4 brush, paint in the details, using charcoal grey for outlining and following the colors in the photograph (front door: dark salmon; back door and planter: mustard; window panes: cream; stones: blue grey; woodpile: medium brown). Highlight stonework and planks with cream.

Name Scroll and Sconces

1. Write the cottage owner's name on a strip of antique-look paper 3" by ½" (8 by 1:5cm) (Or, to antique your own: Mix a droplet of brown paint with some decoupage medium, paint both sides of the paper, and let dry.) Glue half a toothpick to each end and let dry. Roll ends around toothpicks and glue, following the photo.

2. For sconces, roll up two 1" (2.5cm) square papers to form cones. Glue, and paint charcoal grey. Trim tops flat and glue to stone trim, as in photo, spaced so that the toothpick scroll will slide in. Glue as needed.

Foliage, Flowers, and Finishing

1. With a damp sea sponge, dapple in foliage, working from dark green at the lowest level to medium green, apple green, and mustard. The colors should blend a little—no need to dry between colors.

2. With #1 or #2 brush, paint in flowers (here, cream with orange centers and salmon with cream).

3. Clean up any stray pencil lines with vinyl eraser. Apply three coats of acrylic varnish or decoupage medium to entire inside and outside of pot. Apply two coats of polyurethane to the inside of the pot.

Sometimes when history repeats itself, it's good news. Terra-cotta pots are a hot item today among cooks on the cutting edge, just as they were for many centuries B.F. (before flowerpots).

According to Walter Potenza, chef-owner of La Locanda del Coccio (the Inn of Clay) in Providence, Rhode Island, "Cooking in rough clay is the oldest method of cooking in the world." Potenza, a native Italian, introduced terra-cotta cookery to his customers in 1994. In New York City's East Village restaurant Circa, chef Frank DeCarlo also offers diners flavorful terra-cotta-baked dishes. "Anything that's in the pot will marry," De Carlo says. "All the ingredients will marry together and create something really nice."

"When you cook with unglazed terra-cotta," Potenza advises, "you must soak the pot in water for a minimum of fifteen minutes. We prepare individual dishes, bite-sized pieces of chicken or lamb with rice, beans, arranged in layers in circular patterns...perhaps in a fish-based broth, or clam juice. No fat at all."

Baked in a hot oven, the terra-cotta releases its moisture and bastes the food. "The water imparts a taste of ancient days to the food—a warm, comforting, soothing flavor feeling," Potenza explains. Just before serving, he sometimes "drizzles a little olive oil on top, to give a flavor-sense of olive." He serves the food in its terra-cotta baking dish; diners can eat straight out of the pot if they want to.

Potenza has done his homework on terra-cotta cooking in Italy. "The Etruscans, around where Rome is today, central Italy, cooked in clay, over charcoal or wood," his research shows. "Then cooking in clay was popular in the Middle Ages in Tuscany. The servants cooked in clay, but the nobility cooked in cast iron. By the end of the Renaissance, the method had become even more popular, especially around Florence."

Potenza has his pots custom made at the Old Saybrook Pottery Place in Sharon, Connecticut, where Paula Bush-Mette says they are made just like ordinary terra-cotta flowerpots—unglazed, wheel-thrown. The cooking pots are about 1½" deep and 8" or 10" in diameter, Bush-Mette says. Could someone cook in a regular flowerpot? "People do," Bush-Mette says. "But for the rest of us besides Walter who haven't really cooked in terra-cotta, I would go with glazed pots."

Potenza said to clean the cooking pots, one should not use soap (the clay would absorb it), just scrub and sterilize in water 160° to 170 ° in a dishwasher.

If you're ready to try your hand at terra-cotta cooking, you can find the pots at housewares and cooking specialty stores.

Pasticcio, one of Walter Potenza's savory casseroles, baked pasta layered with meat and vegetables in a terra-cotta pot.

Frank DeCarlo's Bocconcini

An appetizer for four: mozzarella cheese wrapped in prosciutto and baked in a terra-cotta pot.

¼ lb. prosciutto
½ lb. mozzarella, cubed
1 tsp. olive oil
Herb/Parmesan bread crumbs
Basil

Wrap cubes of mozzarella in prosciutto and place them in the pot. Sprinkle with a little virgin olive oil and bake for a few minutes until soft. Then top with a little herb bread crumbs. Place back in the oven at 550° for 30 seconds until nicely browned. To serve, add a sprig of fresh basil.

Batik Musicians and Trees

DESIGNER: DANA IRWIN

These pots owe part of their distinction to the faux-batik technique they're made with—instead of fabric, dye, and wax, it calls for clay, paint, and liquid resist medium from a craft-supply store. At least half the fun comes with the magical exposure of the terra-cotta design as the medium is rubbed off.

MATERIALS

Liquid frisket, masking liquid,
or rubber cement

Paintbrushes

Paint pen

Acrylic paint

Water

Art gum eraser

WHAT TO DO

1. Select the design you wish to copy onto the pot. Stencils work fine with this technique.

2. Paint the design onto the pot with a brush or pen dipped in liquid frisket or other resist liquid. The frisket acts as a resist to the acrylic paint you will use on the rest of the pot.

3. When the frisket has dried, paint the pot with slightly watered-down acrylics. Cover the entire pot with paint and let dry.

4. Rub the frisket off of the pot with an eraser or your finger. The natural terra-cotta will show through in the image you originally painted on.

DESIGNER'S TIPS

❧ Finding images you like for your pot is an adventure in itself. This musician pot was inspired by images of Peruvian musicians painted on a gourd from South America.

❧ Although rubber cement works for this process, it is more crude than other resist liquids.

❧ For small details and lines you may want to use a paint pen, or a piece of bamboo sharpened to a point at one end.

Gilded Elegance

DESIGNER: ELLEN ZAHOREC

Whether they're glittering by candlelight, reflected in mahogany, or shining on a sunny window sill, these handsome Long Tom pots (for plants that appreciate root room) make a striking statement—just the gift for the friend who has everything (or hardly anything).

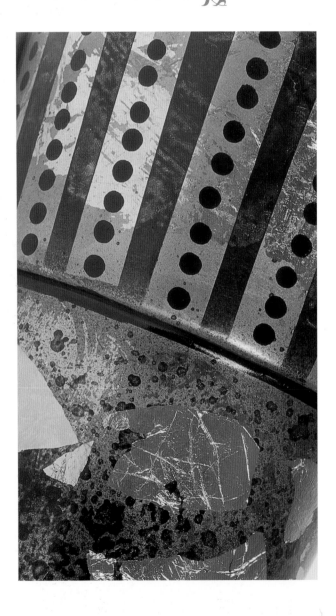

MATERIALS

Long Tom terra-cotta pots

Gold spray paint

Composition gold foil

Cellophane tape

Black spray paint

Gold enamel paint pen

Paintbrush

Polyurethane sealant

Note: You'll find composition gold foil at craft stores.

WHAT TO DO

1. Spray paint the pots gold inside and out, and while the paint is still wet, press on thin gold foil. Let dry completely.

2. With cellophane tape, mask out stripes, then lightly spray paint black. Let dry.

3. Gently remove tape and add dots with enamel paint pen. **Safety warning: When using an enamel paint pen, be sure the room is well ventilated; the fumes are toxic.**

4. Add more gold foil until you get the effect you like.

5. Finish by brushing on polyurethane sealant.

POT SHOT

The first plant collectors we know about were Egyptian soldiers about 3,500 years ago. They are depicted in the Temple of Karnak bringing back 300 plants to pharoah Thothmes III as booty from a Syrian campaign. Another and related first: Terra-cotta soldiers were first planted in China about 2,200 years ago by China's first emperor, Qin Shi Huang Ti, in Xian, southwest of Beijing.

Ancient Paint

DESIGNER: SHEILA ENNIS-SHULZ

This stunning pot seems to have spent its life on a sunny Italian terrace, foaming with bougainvillea. In fact, you control the aging, and a glaze does the coloring. You can find joint compound at hardware stores, glazing medium at paint stores, tints at art supply stores. This pot is worth the shopping trip. ✄

MATERIALS

Joint compound
Foam brush
Paper towels
Water-based glazing medium
Green and yellow tints
Paintbrush

WHAT TO DO

1. Apply the joint compound with a foam brush or your hands.
2. When the compound begins to dry, dab off some areas of the compound with a dry paper towel—this gives the pot the peeled-paint look. Let dry overnight.
3. Apply glaze with a paintbrush in the colors you have selected.

POTS OF A CERTAIN AGE

As with wine and human beings, so with terra-cotta pots. For the connoisseur, age only adds to their character and beauty. One of the problems with waiting around for a terra-cotta pot to age to perfection is that it might break before it gets there, especially if you live in a cold climate. The aging process speeds up outdoors. A related problem is, of course, time. You might want an aged-looking pot now.

I know of three ways to age pots fast, other than putting them in a small enclosed space with a crowd of adolescent pots. The methods are crackling, paint "peeling," and the yoghurt treatment.

Two projects in this book give instructions for painting pots with crackle medium—the Antique Ivy and the Hobbit Cottage pots. You can easily see the results in the project photos—as if the paint had cracked all over from age. The project called Ancient Paint uses joint compound to give the impression of old, peeled paint, leaving a lovely uneven ancient-looking surface.

Finally, the yoghurt method, whose moss-like results you see in the accompanying photo. To try this, you'll

Pots "aged" by brushing on joint compound, treating with yoghurt, and painting on crackle medium.

need a terra-cotta pot and these materials:

- White craft glue
- 8 oz. (240ml) of yoghurt
- Sand
- Paintbrush
- Cheesecloth or paper towels
- Plastic bag
- Spray bottle and water

Paint the outside of the pot with white glue and roll it in sand, or sprinkle a generous layer of sand on it. Let dry for about an hour, then gently brush off the excess sand. Paint the pot thick with yoghurt. Wrap the pot in damp cheesecloth or paper towels and put it in a plastic bag. For about two weeks, keep the pot in a warmish, dim place (say, a kitchen cupboard) and spray it with water whenever you think of it. If left in the dark past three weeks, the growth will continue, but the pot will begin to smell—and not like flowers.

Pot aged naturally, with markings from watering with hard water.

57

Fabric Decoupage

DESIGNER: ELLEN ZAHOREC

This elegant pot seems destined to hold evening primroses or perhaps white orchids—something that breathes romance and candlelight. Create a different mood simply by varying the fabric—the perfect solution for that scrap box full of brocades, crushed velvets, and ginghams.

MATERIALS

Terra-cotta pot

Fabric (enough to cover the pot plus some)

Scissors

Spray adhesive

Paintbrush

Polycrylic finish

Velvet French-wire ribbon (enough to wrap around the rim of the pot)

8" (21cm) of ¼" (1cm) gold metallic braid

Hot-glue gun and glue sticks

WHAT TO DO

1. Cut the fabric into small pieces.
2. Spray the pot with adhesive and apply the pieces of fabric, overlapping the edges.
3. Brush on a clear, polycrylic finish.
4. Use a hot-glue gun to glue the velvet ribbon in several places around the rim of the pot. Be careful when working with the hot glue, for the metal in the ribbon will absorb the heat and burn bare fingers. Overlap the ends of the ribbon and glue.
5. With 2" (5cm) lengths of metallic braid, crimp the ribbon in three or four places evenly spaced around the pot. To create a "swag" effect, wrap the braid around the ribbon, then pinch it together slightly to crimp the ribbon. Twist the ends of the braid together and glue them to the pot, behind the ribbon.

Take It for Granite

DESIGNER: ELLEN ZAHOREC

This pot's faux-granite texture is not only a novel surface treatment but handsome on its own or as a striking background for any bright color and design. You simply spray it on, then play with the "puff" paint.

MATERIALS

Terra-cotta pot

Dark shade of acrylic spray paint

Faux-granite decorative spray paint

Pencil

Paintbrush

Squeeze bottles of dimensional paint
(here, light blue and turquoise)

Polycrylic sealant

Note: If your water-soluble faux-granite paint comes with an accompanying spray can of sealant, as is often the case, you don't need additional sealant. You can find this decorative paint in hardware, craft, and paint stores.

WHAT TO DO

1. Spray the entire pot with a dark undercoat of acrylic paint, and let dry.
2. Spray the outside of the pot with faux-granite paint. While the paint is still wet, scratch a design of your choice in the surface with the end of a paintbrush or the eraser end of a pencil. Let dry.
3. Highlight your design with dimensional ("puff") paint.
4. Spray the entire pot, inside and out, with polycrylic sealant.

POT SHOT

Cultures and individuals (besides you) who have made art from terra-cotta include the ancient Egyptians, between 3500 and 3200 B.C....the Etruscans and the Greeks, around 500 B.C., including Euphronius the Painter, a Greek sculptor whose statue of Heracles wrestling with Antaeus is in the Louvre...Indians in Oaxaca and Anasazi Native American Indians, both in the First century A.D....Luca and Andrea Della Robbia (uncle and nephew) in the 1400s...and Bernini in the 16th century. (You can see some of Bernini's work at the Detroit Institute of Arts and Della Robbia's at the National Gallery of Art in Washington.)

POTTING YOUR PLANTS

To thrive, plants—like people—need a healthy environment. Besides the right location in terms of light, heat, and moisture, they need a suitable container.

Your basic categories of choice are (1) terra-cotta or plastic pots, (2) pot holders, or pot "hiders," and (3) larger containers that hold several pots or plants.

If you're planting one plant in a pot, as a gift or as a specimen plant for your own home, the assumption of this book is that you'll use a terra-cotta pot. Generally speaking, you'll repot a plant you bring home from the nursery or florist in the same size pot it arrives in.

You also have the option of placing the plant in its original pot inside one of your decorated pots as a pot "hider." This should be at least an inch wider than the pot and slightly taller. For cacti and succulents, leave the space between empty. For other plants fill the space with—and stand the pot on—damp peat.

This double-potting method with the layer of damp peat has several advantages for the plant. Because you keep the peat thoroughly moist, it raises the relative humidity around the plant, which keeps plants much happier in winter, especially. It also provides a reservoir of moisture below the pot and insulates the inner potting soil from sudden and harmful temperature changes.

Why Containers?

The great thing about containers, as opposed to smaller individual pots, is they give you more scope for combining plants. (A bulb bowl is the simplest example of this kind of container.) When you bring new plants home, you can either repot them soon afterward into a container as a group, or you can arrange a group of plants in a container, still in their original pots. Anything that will hold water works as a container—an old school desk, a window box, a large flowerpot from this book.

If the container has no drainage capacity, you need to be especially careful with watering. If it's impractical to punch holes in the container, put a ¼" (1cm) layer of small pebbles in the bottom, then a shallow layer of small lumps of charcoal, then potting soil.

Almost all of the potted plants on this sunny patio are double potted. The pot in which they are planted is set inside another, more attractive pot for display.

Ruby and Gold Foil

Designer (and candy eater): Ellen Zahorec

The only drawback to making this glittery candy-wrapper covered pot is that someone has to eat the candy first, and dietetic candy wrappers just don't seem to look as...delicious. Still, it's all in the cause of art. ✃

Materials

Foil candy wrappers

Spray adhesive

Composition gold foil

Paintbrush

Polyurethane sealant

*Note: You'll find composition gold foil
at craft stores*

What to Do

1. Eat the candy, or make someone else eat it. Flatten the foil wrappers.
2. Spray the pot with adhesive and glue the wrappers on.
3. Burnish the foil flat with the side of a brush.
4. Add gold foil to the collar of the pot to get an effect that pleases you.
5. Seal by brushing on polyurethane sealant.

POT SHOT

Here's a psychological tip about gift plants. That gorgeous gloxinia you got for Mother's Day? That charming Valentine's Day cyclamen? That bright birthday chrysanthemum? They're all supposed to die down in a few weeks. Try to think of them as long-lasting cut flowers rather than as failed potted plants. To prolong their lives as long as possible: put them in a very well-lit spot and leave them there.

Faux Mosaic

DESIGNER: JEAN WALL PENLAND

*This bright faux mosaic is a combination of white, green, and turquoise layers—
the painting is as much fun as the finished pot is striking.*

MATERIALS

Terra-cotta pot

White acrylic paint

Paintbrush or foam brush

Bright lime green fabric paint

Turquoise acrylic paint

Alcohol

Cotton balls

Paper towels

Paste floor wax

WHAT TO DO

1. Paint irregular but mostly rectangular shapes on the terra-cotta pot with a paintbrush or foam brush dipped in white acrylic paint. Let dry.

2. Paint the entire pot with two or three coats of lime green fabric paint, allowing it to dry between coats. The finish will be irregularly translucent and not well covered.

3. Paint on a coat of turquoise acrylic paint and allow to dry.

4. With a moistened cotton ball or paper towel, gently remove the turquoise paint from the rectangular areas. Be careful not to remove the intervening layers of lime green paint. Allow to dry.

5. Apply paste floor wax to the outside. Let dry. Polish the pot with a paper towel to get the subtle patina finish.

POT SHOT

For whatever reasons,
you might choose to house plants that
remove pollutants from the air. Here are
some: ivy, aloe, chrysanthemum, the genus
Scindapsis (silver vine, devil's ivy or golden
pothos, etc.), peace lily, and spider plant.

Matisse Dandelion

DESIGNER: CATHY SMITH

This suitably bright ode to the lowly dandelion may inspire you to turn other favorite flowers into contemporary graphics, a nice contrast to the more traditional decoupage motifs. ❧

MATERIALS

8" (21cm) terra-cotta pot

#14 round brush

Opaque yellow and bright blue paper (60 lb.)

Dandelion pattern

Graphite transfer paper

Pencil or pen

Craft knife with very sharp #11 blades

Gloss acrylic decoupage medium (adhesive and sealer)

Oil-base polyurethane

Bright yellow acrylic craft paint or yellow latex interior paint

Turquoise or aquamarine acrylic craft paint (or whatever color matches your paper)

White acrylic craft paint

Water

Mineral oil or turpentine

Small scissors

Tape

WHAT TO DO

1. Paint the outside of the pot with two base coats of white acrylic, allowing the first coat to dry before you apply the second.

2. Apply three coats of yellow acrylic, allowing each coat to dry.

3. Paint blue squares alternating with yellow around the pot rim (or a design of your choice).

4. With transfer paper and pen, trace the dandelion pattern from page 68 onto the back of the blue paper: To keep the pattern from shifting, tape it to the graphite paper and the graphite paper to the blue paper.

5. Cut out the blue dandelion with the craft knife. Don't tear any incompletely cut paper—recut it with the craft knife for a clean separation.

POT SHOT

The common dandelion, *Taraxacum officinale*, which takes a lot of abuse from gardeners and the lawn obsessed, deserves some applause and recognition. Its every part is useful—its flowers make sweet summer wine, its nutritious young leaves flavor salads and teas, and its roots are decocted by herbalists for all kinds of restoratives. It's a survivor, as hardy and bright in concrete cracks as along parched roadsides. In fact, as we know, dandelions owe their survival to children, whose job it is to blow on their feathery seed heads.

6. To glue the cutout design to the pot, apply decoupage adhesive to the pot, covering an area the size of the cutout. Gently lay the cutout on the wet adhesive and smooth down. Repeat on the other side of the pot if you want dandelions on both sides.

7. For the rim decoration, cut out wavy stripes from the blue paper and irregular yellow circles. (Think Matisse!) Glue the stripes and spots around the pot rim with decoupage adhesive.

8. Apply three coats of decoupage medium to the outside of the pot and two coats to the inside (including the bottom). Allow to dry between coats.

9. Apply two coats of polyurethane to the inside of the pot, including the bottom—let it dry between coats.

▰▰▰ DESIGNER'S TIP: ▰▰▰

✿ You can use latex interior for the yellow color, but it is more expensive and has a less smooth finish than acrylic. On the other hand, acrylic yellow requires three coats.

Oriental Orchid Pot

Decorator: Sheila Ennis-Shulz

With a shape designed especially for orchids, this pot's Oriental motif makes it just as apt for these branches of money plant or for elegant arrangements of dried flowers and weeds of all kinds. Or for your chopstick collection.

Materials

Terra-cotta pot

Black spray paint

Craft glue, slightly diluted

Paintbrush

Chinese newspaper

Dark brown stain or water-based wood glaze (dark-brown-tinted glazing medium)

Dark orange raffia

What to Do

1. Spray the pot inside and out wherever you want the black paint to be visible. Spray paint the wooden drawer pulls.
2. Cut the newspaper into strips for wrapping around the pot. Brush the outside of the pot with craft glue and apply the strips of newspaper. Use a brush coated with glue to smooth out any wrinkles in the newspaper. Let dry overnight.
3. Coat the newspaper with glaze or stain and let dry.
4. Glue the raffia trim around the pot, as in the photograph.

Designer's Tip

❊ To find Chinese newspapers, try international newspaper stands and bookstores or Asian food markets.

Stamp,
Stencil,
and Sponge

Antique Ivy Pots

DESIGNER: DOLLY LUTZ MORRIS

Sometimes the contemporary look is the last thing you want. This handsome "antique" crackle finish comes straight out of a can, and you control the amount and placement of the cracking.

MATERIALS

Clay pot

Stencil

Paintbrushes

Acrylic paints

Crackle medium

Spray or brush-on urethane sealer

Gold paint

Antiquing medium

WHAT TO DO

1. How thickly you apply the crackle medium partly determines how much crackling you will have. For dark colors like the red and green pots here, apply crackle medium directly on the pot surface, following the manufacturer's directions for application and drying time. For light colors like the ivory pot here, first apply a base coat of green paint and allow it to dry before applying the crackle medium.

2. Apply the finish coat of paint—it will begin to crackle immediately. You can influence the amount of crackling by how thickly you apply this paint.

3. When the pot is dry, paint on the stencil design. With a dry brush, lightly brush the rim of the pot with gold paint. Apply sealant according to the manufacturer's instructions.

4. To make your pot look even more antique-like, apply antiquing medium, following the manufacturer's instructions, then apply a final coat of sealant.

POT SHOT

For people who are serious about getting into terra-cotta: in 1891 in Ontario, Canada, the village of Salmonville changed its name to Terra-Cotta, probably because of its excellent natural resources. Thick limestone deposits, rich, deep clay, sandstone, and shale attracted brickmaking companies at the turn of the century, turning the little village into a boom town until the Depression struck. Artists and tourists began arriving in the 1940s, and now even the salmon are back in the Credit River.

Vineyard, Strawberries, and Angels

DESIGNER: ELENA LANGE

The designs for these three rather romantic pots, evocative of sun-drenched summer fields and hillsides and of a peaceful cherub-filled paradise, begin at your local crafts store with readymade foam blocks: instant artist.

MATERIALS

For the vineyard pot:

6" or 8" (15 or 21cm) terra-cotta pot and saucer

Small acrylic paintbrush— ¾" or ⅝" (2cm) #10 works well

Grapevine decorator foam blocks

8 oz. (240ml) of water-base sealer, matte finish

2 oz. (60ml) each of pale creamy yellow acrylic paint, ivy-green glaze, and deep purple glaze

Clear acrylic spray, gloss finish

For the strawberries pot:

3 gal. (6.8 l) terra-cotta strawberry pot

Small acrylic paintbrush—¾" or ⅝" (2cm) #10

Berries decorator foam blocks

Newspaper

8 oz. (240ml) of water-base sealer, matte finish

Ivory spray paint, satin finish

4 oz. (120ml) of warm white acrylic paint

2 oz. (60ml) each of: bright red, ivy green, and leaf green glaze

12 oz. (360ml) of clear acrylic spray, gloss finish

For the angels pot:

6" (15cm) terra-cotta pot and saucer

Small acrylic paintbrush—¾" or ⅝" (2cm) #10

Angels and stars decorator foam blocks

8 oz. (240ml) of water-base sealer, matte finish

Red pot: 2 oz. (60ml) each of red and metallic silver

White pot: 2 oz. (60ml) each of off-white and metallic bronze

Newspaper

12 oz. (360 ml) of clear acrylic spray, gloss finish

WHAT TO DO

1. Brush two coats of sealer on the pot (and saucer), inside and outside, allowing it to dry between coats. When the second coat is dry, *for the strawberry pot* line the inside with newspaper to protect it from spray, then spray the outside with two coats of ivory paint, allowing it to dry between coats.

2. *For the strawberry pot:* Apply two or three coats of warm white paint— enough so that the color is opaque— to the entire outside and the upper inside rim of the pot. Allow to dry between coats. *For the vineyard pot:* Apply

There's no rule that you have to paint strawberry pots with strawberries, but it's a tempting notion. To actually plant a strawberry pot with strawberries, you fill it with potting medium, then tuck seedling plants in the various openings, set the pot in full sun, and keep it watered and fertilized until it's aburst with fruit.

As beguiling as these sparkling cherubim are for Christmas pots, they're capable of bringing charm and cheer year round. For heavenly harmony, consider planting your pots with angel's wings (elephant ears), sweet-smelling angel's trumpets, or summer-flowering angel-wing begonia.

four coats of yellow paint to the outside and inner rim of the pot and to the whole saucer. *For the angels pot:* Apply two coats of the base paint to the outside and inner rim of the pot and to the whole saucer. Be sure each coat of paint is dry before you apply the next.

3. To decorate, follow the instructions on the foam blocks package for loading the forms with paint and for applying them so that the pattern doesn't repeat. *For the strawberry pot:* Use the red glaze for the strawberries, and mix the ivy and leaf-green for the leaves. *For the angels pots:* Use the metallics for the angels.

4. Spray the finished pot with sealer; when the first coat is dry, spray a second time.

DESIGNER'S TIP

❀ Working on a cylindrical surface, it's a challenge not to allow the foam blocks to slide and smudge the print. I work with a third to half the pot at a time, laying the pot on its side in my lap to make it easier to press the forms. I don't move on to the next area until the pot is completely dry again.

Stamped Plaids

DESIGNER: MAYA CONTENTO

If plaid pops your cork, you'll love these bright pots for both their design and their amazingly easy technique. Stylish enough to serve chips in at your next casual gathering, colorful enough to bring summer to a wintry room.

MATERIALS

Clean terra-cotta pots and saucers

Acrylic paint in the colors of your choice

Paintbrush

Large rubber art eraser (Select one the width of the area you want to decorate.)

Sharp knife

Clear, waterproof acrylic sealant

WHAT TO DO

1. Paint the inside of the pot in a bright shade of acrylic paint, then paint the outside of the pot and saucer in a contrasting color.

2. Use a sharp knife to cut a plaid pattern into the top of the eraser.

3. Coat the cut side of the eraser with paint.

4. Holding the eraser lengthwise, stamp the pot once around from the top.

5. Paint the eraser a different color. Hold the eraser sideways and stamp over the first layer of prints. You may need to stamp the eraser in two rows to cover the first layer of plaid print.

6. That's it! When the paint is dry, apply a coat of acrylic sealant to the entire pot.

POT SHOT

Keep your plants out of dangerous neighborhoods. Don't put them:

- on the TV or a radiator.
- on a windowsill by a drafty window.
- near a cooling or heating vent.
- between an open window and a door.
- in a poorly lit spot.
- between a window and closed curtains in frosty weather.

Frogs

DESIGNER: MAUREEN S. DONAHUE

A playful combination of stenciled frogs and freehand swirls and dots makes a pot that says both handmade and artful. But if not frogs (although how apt for a flowerpot), perhaps turtles, toads...or leapin' lizards.

MATERIALS

10" (26cm) terra-cotta pot and saucer

Acrylic paint: bronze, burnt sienna, red clay, copper, and black

Stencil material or thick frosted acetate

Dark green fabric paint

Sponge

Water and container for mixing

Old toothbrush

Craft knife

WHAT TO DO

1. Sponge a generous layer of bronze paint onto the pot and saucer and allow to dry.
2. Sponge on layers of burnt sienna, red clay, and copper until you achieve an effect you like.
3. Mix a little black paint with water. Dip an old toothbrush into the mix and flick small dots of black paint onto the pot and saucer.
4. From the stencil material or acetate, cut the frog stencil, using the pattern here. Hold the stencil on the pot and sponge black paint through the stencil to make a frog. Randomly stencil frogs around the pot at different angles.
5. With green fabric paint, add some dots and swirls to the rim in a very loose freestyle pattern. Add a few dots of paint to the rim of the saucer.

Heavenly Herbs: Fragrant Windowsill Gardens

In any kitchen where there's some serious creative cooking going on (this includes combining the contents of several cans, or experimenting with the Sunday-morning scrambled eggs), what's more satisfying than snipping a sprig of sage or a handful of

Identifying herbs by name on their pots is especially helpful for frantic cooks.

fresh basil from the pots on the windowsill?

Among the herbs that will thrive in your kitchen: parsley, creeping thyme, marjoram, parsley, chives, rosemary, chervil, bay, sage, and mint. For plenty of herbs by summer, start with seedlings in the spring. Starting from seeds may be more of a challenge than you need; parsley, for instance, is notoriously difficult to start from seed. Be sure to keep mint in a pot by itself, or it will take over.

Your herbs will be happy with lots of sunshine and a light, fertile, well-drained soil.

Herbs just as content in pots outdoors are mint, sage, thyme, chives, rosemary, and bay. Pick from these regularly to maintain their shape.

For fragrance, plant lavender or rosemary in low pots near the entrance to a patio or deck. As people brush past, the herbs will release their sweet scent.

House Numbers

DESIGNER: PAMELLA WILSON

Doubling as your house number, these pots are twice as functional (as, say, your neighbors'). Plant them with seasonal annuals for a spot of welcoming color above your door or on your doorstep.

MATERIALS

Terra-cotta pots
White and blue enamel spray paint
White and black acrylic paint
Small paintbrushes
Number stencils (optional)

WHAT TO DO

1. Lightly spray the outside of the pots with alternating coats of white and blue enamel, two coats of each color. Finish with a fifth coat of white if you want a lighter shade. Allow to dry between coats.

2. Paint on the numbers in white acrylic, using stencils if you choose to. Outline the numbers in black acrylic.

Copper-Coiled and Glazed

DESIGNER: SHEILA ENNIS-SHULZ

The coiled copper tubing makes this pot a standout. Not to mention the feathers. And the deep aubergine glaze. And the "broken" effect. A gorgeous accent for any room, any decor.

MATERIALS

Dark purple paint

Assorted paintbrushes

Water-based glazing medium

Bronze metallic tint (not oil)

Plastic bag

Spray polyurethane

Flexible copper tubing

Feathers

Note: You'll find glazing medium at paint stores, tint at art supply stores, copper tubing at hardware stores.

WHAT TO DO

1. Paint the entire pot with purple paint.
2. Mix some of the bronze tint with the glaze medium and apply the mixture to the pot with a small brush.
3. To create the "broken" effect, dab the wet glaze with a plastic bag. Let dry.
4. Spray the pot with two coats of polyurethane to protect the finish.
5. Wrap the copper tubing around the pot, beginning at the top. Leave a few inches of tubing free at the beginning, to shape against the rest of the pot. To break off the extra tubing at the end, simply bend it back and forth. Tuck the flattened end under the base of the pot.

6. Decorate with feathers in the open end of the extra tubing at the top of the pot. Bend the tubing so that it lies across the rest of the coils.

DESIGNER'S TIP

❧ You can recycle feathers from an old feather duster, go for a hike with a friend and gather fallen feathers from the ground, befriend the birdkeeper at the local zoo, or raid a friendly farmyard.

Variations on a Theme

DESIGNER: JEAN WALL PENLAND

These three colorful pots all start with the same two steps—an acrylic base coat, then squeezed-on fabric paint. Each goes on to sing its own artistic song, the result of varied but quite simple printing techniques that produce subtly different and harmonic effects.

Lemons and Limes

MATERIALS

Terra-cotta Pot

White acrylic paint

Paintbrush

Squeezable yellow and green acrylic fabric paints or acrylic paint and squeeze bottles or toothpicks

Complementary shade of acrylic paint for inside of pot

Compressed sponge sheets

Water

Scissors

Note: You can find compressed sponge sheets at craft stores and in craft sections of department stores.

What to Do

1. Paint the entire pot with white acrylic paint. Let dry.
2. With squeezable fabric paint or acrylic paint, draw vertical lines on the pot, following the photo, if you wish. Let dry. (If you are not using squeeze bottles, draw the lines with toothpicks.)
3. Cut half-lemon and half-lime shapes out of the compressed sponge sheets. Soak them in water, press out the excess, and allow to dry.

4. With a brush, apply paint to the now expanded cut sponge shapes and press them to the pot. (Wash the sponges immediately after you are through, for acrylic paint dries rapidly and permanently.)
5. When the lemons and limes have dried, you may want to add accents with the remaining fabric paint.
6. Paint the inside of the pot with a bright, contrasting color of acrylic paint.

Orange with Accents

Materials

Terra-cotta pot

Orange acrylic paint

Squeezable bottles of neon orange, green, purple, and white acrylic fabric paint

Small wooden dowels, round ended and square ended (or any object that will stamp the shapes you want)

What to Do

1. Paint the whole pot with two coats of orange acrylic paint, allowing it to dry between coats. (You may decide to leave the pot its original terra-cotta color, as the orange acrylic changes it only very subtly.)
2. Use squeeze bottles of paint to make circles, triangles, and irregular open shapes on the pot.
3. When the painted shapes have dried, brush paint on the end of a dowel (or whatever you're using for a stamp) and print dots and dashes over the shapes.

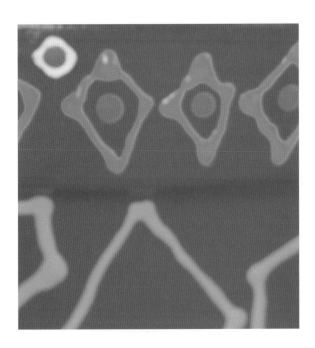

Blue and Purple

Materials

White acrylic paint or latex

Paintbrush

Squeeze bottle

Gesso

Blue and purple fabric paint
or thinned acrylic paint

Paper towels or rags

Paste floor wax (optional)

Note: Craft and art supply stores stock gesso, a primer.

What to Do

1. Paint the entire pot with white acrylic paint.

2. Fill a squeeze bottle with gesso and apply linear shapes to the pot. Let dry. You can paint a layer of white acrylic over the shapes to soften them a bit, if you like.

3. Working with one small area at a time (about 3" or 8cm square), color-stain the pot: brush on a layer of fabric paint or thinned acrylic paint and immediately wipe off with paper towels or rags, so that an irregular translucent layer of paint color remains. For the pot in the photograph, use blue on the lower part of the pot, then purple around the rim.

4. When the pot is dry, you may want to apply paste floor wax to protect the paint and leave a subtle sheen.

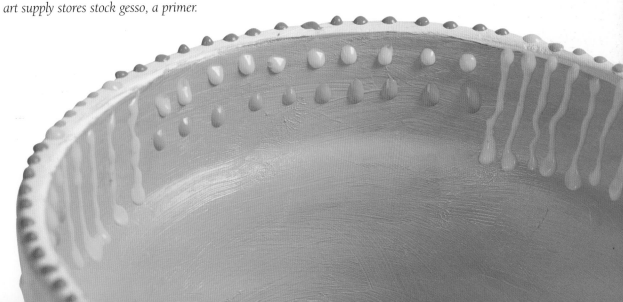

3-D Dots and Dragonflies

DESIGNER: MAUREEN S. DONAHUE

A pot that celebrates whimsy, play, and the incredible lightness of being. Its purple dragonflies (rubber stamped) seem to float through pastel-tinged air...and the colorful polka-dot knobs are there for a very good reason—fun.

MATERIALS

8½" (22cm) terra-cotta pot and saucer

Eleven 1¼" (3.5cm) wooden knobs
(balls with a flat side)

Six to eight colors of acrylic paint

Medium-grade sandpaper

At least four colors of fabric paint

Heavy-duty adhesive sealant

Paintbrush

Rubber stamp (here, a dragonfly)

1. Paint the pot and saucer with random patches of color all over. Paint all 11 knobs with the same colors. Allow to dry overnight.

2. Brush the entire pot and saucer with a coat of acrylic paint (here, ivory). Put dots of contrasting colors of fabric paint on the knobs. Let dry overnight.

3. Sand the (ivory) paint off the pot and saucer until the patches of color show through.

4. Glue the knobs evenly spaced around the rim of the pot.

5. Apply the paint color of your choice to the rubber stamp and stamp randomly all over the pot and saucer.

POT SHOT

What can one put in pots besides plants?
Depending on the size:

- Artificial or dried flowers
- Artists' brushes, pens, pencils
- Change
- Chopsticks
- Christmas-tree balls
- Corks
- Cotton balls
- Fairy lights
- Feathers
- Fireplace spills or long matches
- Gardening tools
- Hand towels
- Hard candies (wrapped)
- Magazines
- Mail
- Marbles
- Napkins
- Pinecones
- Soaps
- Wooden spoons, whisks

Arizona Lizards and Cactus

DESIGNER: PAMELLA WILSON

With their muted sunset background and lively lizards, these pots evoke the Southwest of sidewinders, Georgia O'Keeffe cattle skulls, and the giant saguaro— just the home for these miniature cactus specimens.

MATERIALS

Terra-cotta pots

White and red spray enamel paint

Neon orange and yellow-green acrylic paint

Small paintbrush

Lizard, cactus, or other stencil (optional)

Pencil

WHAT TO DO

1. Spray alternating coats of white and red enamel, two coats of each color, followed by a final coat of white for a lighter tone. Allow to dry between coats.

2. With a pencil, either stencil on or draw on lizards and cactus freehand. Paint with acrylic paint, following the photograph if you wish.

Sparklers

DESIGNER: ELENA LANGE

Three superimposed layers of paint create the richness and depth of color of these subtly gilded pots, equally at home in an elegant drawing room or a sunny studio-apartment window. The decorative technique is simple: sponge and wait, sponge and wait.

MATERIALS

6" (15cm) terra-cotta pots and saucers

Small acrylic paintbrush—
¾" or ⅞" (2cm) #10 works well

Sea sponge

Masking tape

Newspaper

Jar of water

12 oz. (360ml) of water-base sealer, matte finish

2 oz. (60ml) of acrylic paint in your colors of choice. For the pots pictured:

For the purple:
red-violet (base), black, metallic plum

For the blue:
navy blue (base), licorice, metallic periwinkle blue

For the green:
emerald (base), black, metallic emerald

For the gold:
white (base), metallic champagne,
metallic antique gold

12 oz. (360ml) of clear acrylic spray, gloss finish

WHAT TO DO

1. Apply two coats of sealer to the entire pot and saucer, then two to four coats of the base color to the entire outside and the inner rim of the pot up to the rim and to the entire saucer. (Dark colors may need only two coats, lighter colors three or four.) *Be sure each coat of sealer and paint is dry before you apply the next.*

2. To keep the sponged paint where you want it, tape sections of masking tape along the bottom edge of the inner rim of the pot, along the line of base paint.

3. For the purple, blue, and green pots, use black paint for this step. For the gold pot, use metallic champagne. Pour a small amount of paint onto newspaper. Dampen the sponge and squeeze out excess water. Lightly tap the sponge into the paint and randomly "pounce" the sponge over the base coat on the pot and saucer. Use a light touch and turn the sponge as you work so you vary the pattern. Reload the sponge with paint as you need it. Allow the pot to dry.

4. Repeat step 3 with the appropriate metallic paint. Allow to dry.

5. Spray the pots and saucers with two coats of acrylic finish, allowing them to dry between coats.

THE GENEROSITY OF BULBS: SCENT AND COLOR

Indoors or out, bulbs are among the easiest flowering plants to grow, and among the most rewarding—if you happen to enjoy color, fragrance, and fairly instant gratification. The blooming period lasts several weeks if the plants are kept cool.

Indoor-Outdoor Bulbs

Frost-hardy spring-flowering bulbs include grape hyacinths, snowdrops, narcissi, hyacinths, crocuses, and tulips. You can either force these bulbs in winter and early spring, or you can plant them in pots outdoors in the fall and bring them inside in the spring as they're about to flower.

Paper-white narcissi, Dutch hyacinths, and crocuses are sure bets for forcing indoors.

Through late fall and early winter, buy and plant bulbs especially prepared for forcing. (Or refer to one of the many plant and gardening books that contain directions on how to prepare your own bulbs for forcing, which involves planting, darkness, and cold over several months.) Over a layer of pebbles or broken pot

Dutch hyacinths forced from bulbs flourish indoors all winter.

pieces, plant the bulbs close together in a container with excellent drainage (too-damp bulbs will rot). They should not touch each other or the sides of the container. The tips of the bulbs should just break the surface of the potting mixture. Although I've grown bulbs in ordinary potting soil, a special bulb mix is recommended; check with your garden store.

To have flowering plants all winter, plant bulbs every week or two. Let them grow in plenty of light but not sun. Keep the potting soil moist, and feed them with liquid fertilizer. Grape hyacinth and Siberian squill will bloom spring after spring in the same pot for several years. The rest of these bulbs won't bloom again indoors; you can transplant them outside or donate them to a bulb-loving neighbor.

Indoor Bulbs

Plants that flower from bulbs that can't tolerate frost—like begonias and gloxinias—are simply left in their pots when the foliage dies down; you keep their potting mix almost dry until they begin growing again, storing them in some out-of-the way indoor spot. If you plan better than most people, you can have color from these plants all year round.

Bulbs are perennial optimists—they will flower year after year. Among the many plants you can grow from bulbs: amaryllis, belladonna lily, freesia, spider lily, tuberose, and calla lily. Check with your local nursery.

Indoor-Outdoor Bulbs

Bulb Type	Plant In	To Bloom In
Paperwhite, soleil d'or, and geranium narcissi	August-October	December-January
Darwin and lily-flowered tulips	September-October	April
Crocuses	Autumn	January-February
Lily of the Valley	October-November	December-February
Winter aconite	September	January
Snowdrop	September	January
Glory of the snow	September	February
Grape hyacinth	September	January-March
Dutch hyacinth	September-October	Christmas-March
Dwarf iris (*try iris histrioides major, I. reticulata, I. danfordiae*)	September	January-February
Bluebells (*Scilla siberica, S. adlamil, S. violacea*)	September-October	January-March

Bas Relief

Living Leaves

DESIGNER: PERRI CRUTCHER

This leaf-bedecked pot owes its natural beauty to nature and its simple elegance to human design. Although the magnolia and camelia leaves here complement each other perfectly, you can substitute any glossy, sturdy leaves. With an artful arrangement of fresh flowers, this pot makes a stunning centerpiece or gift.

MATERIALS

Terra-cotta pot

Magnolia and gardenia leaves

Gold-wrapped wire cord

Florist's gum

Jar that fits inside pot

Fresh flowers

Water

WHAT TO DO

Simplicity itself. Glue the leaves in layers around the pot, as the photograph shows, with florist's gum (an adhesive). Tie an artful bow with gold-wrapped wire cord, available at florists and craft stores. Fill the jar generously with fresh flowers, add water, and set inside the pot.

Bugle-Bead Trim

DESIGNER: NANCY McGAHA

Simple elegance. A striking combination of the natural pot and a geometric loomed bead design...great for beginning beaders... and the perfect last-minute gift (yet still handmade!).

MATERIALS

4" (10cm) terra-cotta pot
Small bugle beads in your choice of colors
Beading thread
Beading needles
Heavy-duty adhesive
Sewing needle and thread

WHAT TO DO

1. Measure around the rim of your pot to figure out the size of your beading loom—this pot measured 14½" (37cm). For this collar, you'll bead two pieces 7¼" (18.5cm) each on a small loom, 8" x 10" (21 x 26cm), and sew the ends together.

2. On your loom, follow the beading pattern on page 104 or graph your own design on bead-work paper. Reading the graphed design from left to right, you'll string beads from each row of the design onto your needle, one at a time.

3. To loom one piece, thread your beading needle and knot the other end of the thread to the last warp thread on the left of the loom. Following the graph, string the first row of beads onto your needle. Hold the entire threaded row behind the warp threads on your loom, then

OVERCOMING FEAR OF FAILURE: 10 TOP THINGS TO DO ABOUT A POT THAT FAILS

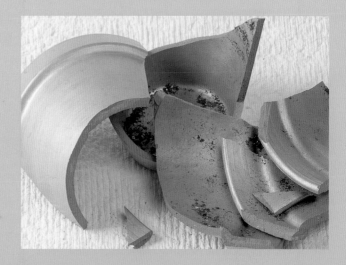

10. Break it up and use it for drainage material in pots that didn't fail.

9. Put something in it that will take the focus off it. Perhaps something semi-illegal.

8. Blame the directions, the materials, the weather, the phase of the moon, or all of these.

7. Give it to someone who doesn't know any better. Or who will love it anyway, like your mother.

6. If it's a painted pot, decoupage it. If it's a decoupaged pot, paint over it. If it broke, glue it back together and then decoupage it. Or antique it. Or both.

5. Bury it.

4. Say it's the latest look (or technique or trend) and reflects contemporary chaos or modern-day angst. Or both.

3. Put it on a very high shelf, behind things. In the garage.

2. Say it was an experiment and you, for one, are not afraid to try new things or to admit it when something doesn't work out. Then bury it.

1. Say someone else made it, perhaps a small child who has moved away.

MAKING A SIMPLE BEADING LOOM

To make your own beading loom for this project, you'll need an 8" x 10" (21 x 26cm) wood picture frame or stretcher frame and push pins. Position four push pins evenly spaced on two sides of the frame. Wrap beading thread around one side of the frame enough times to secure it, then begin wrapping the thread around the pins, back and forth across the frame twice, ending with eight threads—two warp threads per pin. (If you're designing your own pot collar, be sure to thread your beading loom with one thread more than your design calls for—for example, this design is seven beads across so you have eight threads.) At the end, wrap the thread around one side of the frame again and tie it to the beginning of the thread to secure it. Whenever you're knotting the thread, use a square knot when possible.

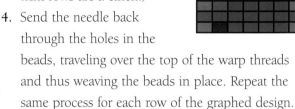

pop the beads into place so that a warp thread lies between each bead. (Once you've done this row, the next rows are a cinch.)

4. Send the needle back through the holes in the beads, traveling over the top of the warp threads and thus weaving the beads in place. Repeat the same process for each row of the graphed design.

5. When you've woven the last row of beads, to lock your thread: Weave only your thread as for the next to last row, from left to right, then as for the last row from right to left—you've made a circle of thread.

6. To tie off each piece, cut the warp threads close to the push pins to leave yourself as much thread as possible to work with. Tie the warp threads together, two or four at a time, in square knots. Clip excess thread.

7. Sew the ends of the two pieces together to form a circle. Slide the circle onto the pot rim and glue in place.

DESIGNER'S TIP

❀ I hold the loom in my lap vertically, so that it's easy to work around.

EMPEROR QIN'S TERRA-COTTA ARMY

China's self-declared first emperor, Qin Shi Huang, "wanted an army with him after he died," says Yuan Zhongyi, the director of the Museum of Terra-Cotta Warriors and Horses outside the Chinese city of Xian. "His underground empire was a miniature of his real one."

In 1974, Yuan and other archaeologists began unearthing that long-rumored underground empire, a great terra-cotta army of some 8,000 life-size figures buried near Qin's tomb more than 2,000 years ago. Qin commissioned the modeling from terra-cotta of rank upon rank of archers, cavalry troops, charioteers, infantrymen, and horses, an undertaking it took 700,000 laborers 36 years to complete.

The size of the tomb complex compares in area to Cambridge, England's—22 square miles. Qin is the same man who commissioned the building of the Great Wall of China and standardized the country's weights and measures, written language, and currency. He also ordered destroyed all books in China except those on his favorite topics, and executed 460 scholars whom he suspected of sabotaging his search for eternal life.

Today, the terra-cotta figures he commissioned fill three enormous pits in the museum. Of the 6,000 soldiers in Pit I, workers have restored 1,000, which now stand four abreast in battle array. Since each figure's face is distinctive, we know they were not only individually sculpted but modeled to represent thousands of different men—along with their idiosyncratic expressions of pride, ferocity, humor, and so on. It's this realism that sets the figures apart from other contemporary art.

The figures in Qin's army were molded of terra-cotta for the most pragmatic of reasons—the clay was handy, along with the wood to fire it.

Soldiers in the terra-cotta army of China's first emperor, who had them buried two millenia ago to protect his tomb.

Mosaics

DESIGNER: TERRY TAYLOR

Make these handsome mosaics from broken china or from dinner plates you find at the flea market or garage sales. Shallow pots like this burgundy mosaic are especially designed for planting bulbs.

MATERIALS

Plates (6-8 plates will cover at
least one 12" [31cm] pot)

Unused terra-cotta pot

Black marking pen

Ceramic tile adhesive

Ceramic tile grout

Tile nippers

Disposable plastic knife or palette knife

Flat packing foam, sponge, or rags for wiping

Containers for mixing grout

Latex gloves

Safety glasses

Safety tip: Always wear safety glasses when you use tile nippers. (You can find inexpensive plastic glasses at hardware stores.)

WHAT TO DO

1. Draw your design on the pot with a marking pen, if you wish.
2. To cover the rim of the pot, you'll use only the outside edges of the plates. With the tip of the tile nippers, nip through the plate edge and trim the plate rim from the bottom of the plate. Set aside the bottom. For finished pieces ½" (1.5cm) wide to fit along the rim of the pot, make nips along the plate edge about ½" to ¾" (1.5-2cm) apart. When you have a pile of pieces, cut them to about ½" (1.5cm) wide.
3. One piece at a time, butter the back with a little tile adhesive, line up the outside edge of the piece with the upper edge of the pot, and stick it on, following your design plan. Trim pieces to fit. Continue until you have a row around the entire edge of the pot. Then repeat with a second row, aligning the pieces with the lower edge of the pot rim.
4. Make small "tiles" from the rest of the plate, the flatter the better, and glue them to the pot in the same way, according to your design.
5. Fill in the spaces between pieces with tile grout. Spread the grout on with packing foam (or a sponge or rag) and push it into the spaces between the tiles, wiping off excess as you go.
6. Let the grout dry for about 15 minutes, then wipe the surface of the tiles clean with a rag. Let the grout dry for about 30 more minutes and wipe the tiles clean with a damp rag. Allow the pot two or three days to dry completely.

DESIGNER'S TIPS

❀ The advantage of using flat packing foam for wiping the grout is that I can break off a small piece, work with it, then throw it away.

❀ If you're planning to leave large spaces between the tiles, I recommend using sanded floor grout rather than wall grout—it comes in various colors. If you use wall grout, you must place the tiles close together.

Nightscape

DESIGNER: MAYA CONTENTO

Whether this striking one-of-a-kind pot reminds you of moonlit landscapes or the night woods, it's an evocative attention grabber and offers endless scope for variations in color and theme—a cityscape at dawn, for instance, or simple palms and grass silhouettes at sunset. ❧

MATERIALS

Terra-cotta pot

Acrylic paint

Acrylic sealant

Paintbrush

Mobile-home metal skirting

Sharp-tip permanent marker

Tin snips

Leather work gloves

Heavy-duty waterproof adhesive

Note: You'll find the mobile-home skirting and the adhesive at home-improvement centers.

WHAT TO DO

1. Paint the pot in a nighttime-dark color to contrast with the silver metal, and let dry.

2. Seal the entire pot, inside and out, with acrylic sealant.

3. With the marker, draw your pattern on the metal—you want to be able to cut the whole pattern in one piece. Whatever your design, be sure to extend the lower edge an extra inch to turn under the pot. For the pattern shown here, measure against your pot so that the moon will attach to the pot rim and the bottom of the trunks will turn under the pot bottom. Attach the full moon to the branches of one tree, and make the trunks extra long.

4. **Safety note: Wear leather work gloves when working with the metal.** Be sure to cut off the lit-tle barbs that form as you snip, so they don't cut you. Cut your pattern out with tin snips.

5. Bend the bottom inch of the tree trunks back to a 90° angle. Attach the bent section to the bottom of the pot with heavy-duty adhesive. Use the adhesive to attach the back of the moon to the pot rim and the trunks to the pot. Let dry, according to adhesive directions.

DESIGNER'S TIPS

❀ The mobile-home metal skirting comes in large sheets, which I had the store cut down to manageable size for me.

❀ Working with metal requires a great deal of care—thus the work gloves. Beware of sharp edges!

POT SHOT

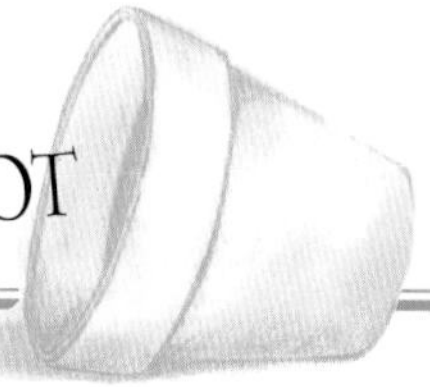

It never hurts to have a little arcane floral knowledge at your disposal in case you're caught in a conversation with some know-it-all plant person. For example, the moisture-loving *azalea*'s name comes from the Greek word for "dry." Two popular plants named after men? *begonia* (Michael Begon, Canadian governor in the 18th century) and *fuchsia* (Leonhart Fuchs, 16th-century German physician and botanist). From the Latin we have *impatiens* (take a guess; its ripe seed pods burst and eject seeds when touched) and *monstera* ("monstrous," but no one knows why).

Southwestern Sand Painting

DESIGNER: CATHY SMITH

Especially appropriate for this Southwest motif, sand painting offers the same grand scope for pot designers as paint, but with the textured look of—well—sand.

MATERIALS

10" (26cm) terra-cotta pot

Decorator sand in 4 oz. (120ml) applicator bottles (yellow, turquoise, white, black)

Matte-finish acrylic decoupage medium

Polyurethane (oil base)

White charcoal pencil or lead pencil

Vinyl eraser

Round brushes: #4 and #1 or #2

1½" (4cm) bristle brush (for sealant)

Hair dryer (if you're in a hurry)

Toothpicks

Cookie sheet or newspaper

WHAT TO DO

1. Clean the flowerpot with a damp cloth

2. Draw the pattern you want with charcoal pencil or lightly in lead pencil.

3. Follow "Painting with Sand" directions, and repeat the process area by area.

4. After all designs are thoroughly dry, erase stray pencil lines and brush away loose sand.

5. With the bristle brush, triple coat the entire outside of the pot with decoupage medium, allowing it to dry between coats. Double coat the inside of the pot.

6. Apply two coats of polyurethane to the inside (including bottom) of the pot.

PAINTING WITH SAND

- To apply the sand, work from light to dark colors. Sand paint patterns in vertical 4" (10cm) stripes. Use one color at a time and work with an area 2" (5cm) square. Use a larger brush for larger areas, a smaller brush for outlining and details.

- Acrylic medium dries fast, so be ready to apply sand as soon as you've applied the medium on the area to be sand painted. Sprinkle sand on the wet medium—push stray sand into place with toothpicks. Allow the sand coat to dry. For good coverage you need three coats of medium and sand—the second and third coats go much faster than the first. By catching excess sand on a newspaper or cookie sheet, you can recycle it.

- Before handling your finished piece, allow the triple-coated areas to dry completely.

DESIGNER'S TIPS

❀ Don't spend much on brushes for sand painting and don't use your good brushes—sand paint destroys them.

❀ Sand paint is fragile and easily damaged when it's wet, but sturdy as rock when dry.

Faux Dirt

Make this earthy dessert delight to brighten a dull winter day, send your favorite kids into giggle spasms, or serve up to guests with a sense of humor (maybe fellow pot decorators). It's a quick-mix dish made of chocolate cookies, gooey stuff, and gummy worms. You might want to introduce it by casually nibbling at the "dirt" or smacking your lips over a worm—then scoop out trowelsful for everyone.

What's for dessert? Dirt!

DIRT DESSERT RECIPE

Adapted by Heather S. Smith

Ingredients and Tools

One 6" (16cm) terra-cotta pot (unused and washed)

Aluminum foil

Masking tape

Large mixing bowl

Fork, whisk, or electric mixer

Package of instant chocolate pudding mix, approximately 3.9-4.25 oz. (110-120g)

1¾ cups (414ml) of reduced-fat milk or milk substitute

2 cups (474ml) of dessert whipped topping

20-25 chocolate sandwich cookies

1 thick plastic food-storage bag

Candy gummy worms, enough for each guest and to decorate the pot

Bright, showy, fresh or fake flowers

Trowel

Directions

Line the inside of the terra-cotta pot with aluminum foil. Use a double layer in the bottom to prevent its being torn by serving utensils. Use tape between the layers of foil and the pot to keep the lining in place. Set aside.

Put the chocolate cookies in a plastic bag and pound them into crumbs. Line the bottom of the pot with a thin layer of cookie crumbs and set the rest of the crumbs aside.

In a large bowl, combine milk and pudding mix. Stir rapidly with a fork or whisk or mix with electric mixer until smooth and creamy. Blend in 1 cup of the whipped topping.

Presentation is all—including artfully placed gummy worms.

Spoon half of the pudding into the pot. Shake some of the remaining cookie crumbs onto the top in a thin layer. Spread the remaining whipped topping over the cookie layer. Spoon the rest of the pudding on top. Fill the rest of the pot with chocolate cookie crumbs so that the finished dessert looks like a pot filled with soil.

For best results chill in the refrigerator several hours.

At serving time, stick some flowers into the top of the dessert. If you use fresh flowers, wrap the stems in plastic. Spread gummy worms artfully around the top of the pot. Serve with the trowel. For a special touch, top each serving with a fresh flower and a gummy worm.

Serve a generous trowelful to each guest.

Variations

- For a new-sown grass look, add coconut dyed with green food coloring on top of the cookie crumbs.
- To make a nondairy version of this dessert, mix the powdered instant pudding with soy milk or nondairy creamer and use a nondairy whipped dessert topping.
- For another healthy version, mix the instant pudding with 16 oz. (453.6g) of silken soft tofu in a blender until smooth and creamy; omit the milk. Use the dessert whipped topping only for the layers—delete the cup blended with the pudding mix. The mixture will be the consistency of pudding, and the tofu will absorb the chocolate flavor. Chill overnight before serving.

Rope and Wood

DESIGNER: SHEILA ENNIS-SHULZ

If you're a dab hand with glue, this handsome pot was made for you. You can reproduce its natural earthy look or dye the twine and paint the wood to create your own color statement.

MATERIALS

Terra-cotta pot

White craft glue

Ball of natural twine (not plastic)

Four wooden drawer pulls

Wooden pegs

Wooden plugs in two sizes

Wood stain, walnut shade

Tweezers

Newspaper, paper towels, or rags

High-gloss spray polyurethane

Hot-glue gun and glue sticks

Note: You can find wooden pegs and plugs at hardware stores.

WHAT TO DO

1. Beginning at the bottom of the pot and working upwards two inches at a time, liberally apply craft glue around the pot. Wind the twine tightly around one glue-covered section at a time. Be sure not to leave any gaps between the rows of twine. Let dry overnight.

2. Stain all the wooden parts. You may want to use tweezers to dip the objects directly into the stain, then lay the pieces out on newspaper, paper towels, or rags to dry completely.

3. Spray the dry wooden parts with polyurethane.

4. Use a hot-glue gun to glue the wooden parts to the pot. Glue the wooden drawer pulls to the bottom of the pot to serve as feet.

Arabian Nights

DESIGNER: SHELLEY LOWELL

A magical contemporary pot that cries out for a frivolous, playful spirit in the making. A creative use for this or any pot is to turn it into a necklace or earring tree. Don't let the long materials list put you off— you'll have most of the supplies around your house. And glass/mirror stores often have scraps they would only throw away. You'll find the gauze in craft stores, the gesso in craft or art supply stores.

Materials

8" (21cm) terra-cotta pot

Polyurethane

Sponge paintbrush

Package of gauze impregnated with plaster

Bowl of water

Gesso

Acrylic paint in two or three colors that work together

Beads, stones, sequins, small buttons, small bells, or other little treasures

Broken pieces of mirror, about equal to a 5" x 7" (13 x 18cm) mirror

Heavy-duty adhesive sealant (for use with glass and metal)

White or clear bathroom caulking in a tube with a nozzle

Contact glue or cement

Nail-polish remover

Cotton balls

Small sponges

Tiny brush

Tweezers

Newspaper

Small hammer or pliers

Single-edge razor blade

Heavy cotton or work gloves

What to Do

1. With the sponge brush, coat the entire pot, inside and out, with polyurethane and let dry.
2. Cut the gauze into 18" (46cm) strips. Dip one strip at a time in water, squeeze out excess, and lay the gauze on, starting at the top of the pot and scrunching and pinching as you go. When the pot is covered, let the gauze dry (up to 24 hours).
3. With a clean sponge, sponge the gesso on the gauze. You may need to turn the pot upside down and around to check all angles to be sure it is completely covered with gesso. Let dry.
4. **Safety note: Wear heavy cotton or work gloves when handling the mirror pieces.** To break the mirror pieces: Wrap one mirror piece at a time in newspaper, then whack it gently with a small hammer or the side of a pair of pliers. (Don't hit too hard or the mirror will break in tiny slivers.) Carefully open the paper and pick out the shards you want to use. You need about 20-25 bits of mirror.
5. With pencil, mark the places on the pot you want the mirror pieces to go. Put a blob of the heavy-duty adhesive on the back of the mirror pieces and a blob on their intended positions. Let the adhesive become tacky (about 10 minutes). Then, carefully press the mirror pieces into place. Let dry about 12 hours.
6. Run a small bead of caulking around the edge of each piece of mirror on the pot. (This is so anyone handling the pot won't have shredded fingers.) You may need to blend it into the gauze. Allow to dry for at least two hours before painting.
7. Using the base color of acrylic paint and a clean sponge, sponge the color on. You may need to turn the pot upside down or around to check all angles to be sure it is completely covered with paint. If there are tiny areas the sponge can't get into, drop the paint in with a tiny brush. Let dry.

8. Continue with coats of the second and third colors, allowing the pot to dry between coats.

9. To add the beads, stones, sequins, etc: At hand you'll need the super glue and tweezers, and—to keep your fingers from being permanently glued together—nail- polish remover (which acts as a solvent for super glue), and cotton balls. Glue on the beads and jewels at random.

10. With a single-edge razor blade, scrape off any paint that may have gotten on the mirror pieces.

DESIGNER'S TIP

❀ If you choose to use several shades of color on your pot, you might make the bottom part of pot darker than the top or the other way around. Or you may want the color shading from light to dark as you turn the pot. I used three shades of blue—a blue/aqua mixture for base, aqua for the next layer, and pale aqua for the top coat.

POT SHOT

If you not only admire terra-cotta but want to do something about it, you can join FTC—Friends of Terra Cotta—a New York City-based national nonprofit organization that promotes education about and research for the preservation of architectural terra-cotta. What terra-cotta aficionado could resist their publication titled *Terra Cotta: Don't Take It for Granite* (three walks in NYC)?

Iguana

DESIGNER: SHELLEY LOWELL

This pot will have heads snapping for a second look. If iguanas leave you cold, substitute the pot-climber of your choice, then choose colors that complement your critter. The iguana on this pot came just as it appears, from a toy store. ❧

MATERIALS

8" (21 cm) terra-cotta pot

Acrylic paint in 2 or 3 colors that will work together with the terra-cotta color and the iguana (here, ultramarine, light olive green, dark green, pale yellow green)

Contact glue or cement

A toy replica of an iguana

Chalk or pastel pencil that will show up on your colors

WHAT TO DO

1. Paint your design on the pot, or follow the design in the photograph.

2. Decide where you want to position the iguana and mark off the areas of the body, feet, and tail with chalk. Refer to the cement instructions regarding how much cement to use and how long to wait before attaching the iguana to the pot. Glue on the iguana.

Clay Sun

Designer: Pamella Wilson

Clay in the same terra-cotta shade as the pot gives this sculpted creation a natural look as sunny as its mischievous expression—although you may choose to decorate pot, face, or both with acrylic paint after baking. The sun face bakes in your oven to the same weather-resistant, porous finish as the pot.

Materials

Terra-cotta pot

Oven-bake or polymer clay

Rolling pin

Kitchen knife

Paintbrush or other edging tool

Pencil

Note: You'll find oven-bake or polymer clay at craft stores.

What to Do

1. Roll out a slab of clay ¼" (1cm) thick and cut out a circle that will fit the side of your pot.

2. Lay the circle on the pot and form it to the rounded pot shape. Then sculpt and pinch the facial features or, if you prefer, draw a face on the clay with pencil and incise the features into the clay.

3. Lay the pot down sideways and press the clay circle tight against the pot for drying. The clay must be bone dry before baking.

4. When dry, remove the sun from the pot and bake it according to the instructions on the clay package.

5. Use epoxy or super glue to attach the sun securely to the pot.

Forest Naturals

DESIGNER: JEAN TOMASO MOORE

Half the pleasure in making this pot lies in gathering the materials during a walk or two in the woods or a park. A fern or other "woodsy" specimen planted in the pot becomes a natural extension of its container.

MATERIALS

Terra-cotta pot

Natural materials (plenty of bark)

Sheet moss

Chopstick or paintbrush

Hot-glue sticks and hot-glue gun

WHAT TO DO

1. Working with the pot on a flat surface, start with the bigger pieces of bark. Lay the first piece against the pot, finding its easiest lie against the curvature. Hot glue at the points where it touches the pot.

2. Work around the entire pot with pieces of bark, overlapping the larger pieces and filling in with smaller pieces as you go.

3. As you continue creating your pot, fill in with other natural materials. Remember to keep the base of the pot level, and arrange materials at the top of the pot toward the outside, to leave room for a plant.

4. Fill all remaining gaps with moss, tucking it in with the chopstick or paintbrush end. If you have used branches with jagged edges, tip with hot glue and cover with moss.

5. Hot glue sheet moss around the entire inside top rim, pressing it carefully against the outside materials.

DESIGNER'S TIP

❋ I collected all the natural materials for this pot on a brief but fruitful walk in the woods except the moss and a bit of eucalyptus—bark from fallen trees, twigs, small pine cones, acorns, lichen-covered branches.

Midas Touch

DESIGNER: TERRY TAYLOR

*Not only a very classy pot, but the answer to a flea-market and garage-sale shopper's prayer—
a legitimate reason to comb those fascinating venues for tons of "junk" jewelry.*

MATERIALS

Terra-cotta pot

An overgenerous quantity of buttons and "junk" jewelry—pins, earrings, necklaces, bracelets

Jewelry cutters or wire cutters

Jewelry pliers (flat)

Acrylic modeling paste

Small palette knife or a similar tool

Gesso or acrylic base-coat paint

Acrylic metallic gold paint

Small paintbrushes

Masking tape

Optional: composition leaf (available in gold, silver, copper, etc.) and leafing supplies

WHAT TO DO

1. Remove all pin backs, posts, and findings from the jewelry with wire or jewelry cutters and jewelry pliers. Think about what pieces will work well with each other.

2. Spread a generous amount of acrylic modeling paste about ⅟₁₆" (.25cm) thick on a small area of the pot rim—about 3" (8cm). You'll need to stabilize the pot (with bricks, books, wood blocks, etc.) to keep it from rolling.

3. Spread a generous amount of modeling paste on the back of a piece of jewelry—flat earrings need less, for example, than a large domed brooch. Set it

in place on top of the modeling-paste base—you don't need to push it in. Use the palette knife to remove excess modeling paste around the edges. When you've covered your work area with jewelry, let it dry for 24 hours. Thicker amounts of modeling paste require a longer drying period. Repeat steps 2 and 3 until the pot rim is covered.

4. Tape off areas of the pot you don't want to paint, then coat the jewelry surface with acrylic gesso or base-coat paint. Dab the brush into the nooks and crannies to completely cover the jewelry. Allow to dry.

5. Finish with at least two coats of metallic paint or with composition leaf.

▓▓▓ DESIGNER'S TIPS ▓▓▓

❀ Remember that you always need more jewelry than you expect for a project like this!

❀ Plan on several sessions for this pot—don't try to finish it in a weekend. Work in one small area at a time, and let it dry before you start on the next.

❀ If a flat piece of jewelry will not fit on the pot's curved surface, gently bend the jewelry with your fingers or jewelry pliers. If it breaks, don't fret: Just glue the pieces on anyway.

❀ If you opt for composition leaf as a surface finish, I've found it helpful to use a matching base coat—silver for silver leaf, and so on.

Kid Stuff: Plants for Kids and Their Rooms

Remember sticking toothpicks in an avocado seed so you could set it in a jar on the kitchen windowsill? Remember the anticipation of watching it crack? Of peering inside for the light green shoot, and finding it one morning at last reaching for the light?

Kids still like watching things grow, and the faster the better.

They can start plants the same way, from seeds from their breakfast and dinner plates—besides avocados, they can try oranges, lemons, and papayas. They can also plant raw peanuts and unroasted coffee beans. They need to understand they're not going to end up with a lemon or coffee tree, they're just going to get to watch a lemon plant or a coffee plant grow for awhile. A warm bright windowsill is the perfect site.

Other easy-to-grow plants include some from the Saxifrage family. The most familiar is the spider plant, with its new little "spiders" hanging from the ends of its leggy runners. A similar plant, also with long threadlike runners with "baby plants" at the ends, is called magic carpet or mother of thousands. Another is the piggyback plant, which develops tiny new plants beneath its heart-shaped clusters of leaves. The "offspring" of all three of these plants will root quickly when put into soil. The parent plants do best as hanging plants or in wall brackets (at child's-eye level).

Lots of kids find cacti fascinating—a little desert on their windowsill. They'll love *Gymnocalycium, Notocactus, Mammillaria,* and *Rebutia* (no tougher to learn than Tyrannosaurus, Stegosaurus, and Diplodocus). All produce gorgeous bright flowers and are easy to grow. As desert natives, they thrive on just the kind of neglect some kids are good at—they need a sunny window and grow in a commercial potting medium that resembles desert sand. The only danger is overwatering.

Insect-eating plants fascinate older kids. The catch is that in winter kids may have to go insect hunting to feed their Venus fly traps and pitcher plants. The fly trap is the more dramatic eater: when an insect lands on its leaf tip, the leaf snaps shut around the victim. (Who wouldn't enjoy watching that?) Insects slide to their doom down the slippery, pitcher-shaped leaves of pitcher plants to drown in the plant's digestive juices.

Some children will enjoy sweet-scented flowering bulbs as much as some adults do, especially if they plant them in glass containers so they can watch the growth process. They can try hydroculture on these: plant narcissi or hyacinth bulbs in water-retaining clay granules or gravel, with their tops just visible above the mixture. Add water until it is almost touching the bulbs. (They can also plant these the way you did avocados—suspended on rafts of sticks above water.) The kids will be able to see the roots and shoots growing in a few weeks—not quite an eternity.

The fascination of cacti, along with their hardiness, makes them ideal for kids' rooms.

CONTRIBUTING DESIGNERS

Maya Contento is a professional chef, poet, and primarily print artist in western North Carolina who can't keep up with the orders for her line of sassy potato-print t-shirts.

Jan Cope gets inspired to paint mountain flowerpots by the mountains around her Asheville, North Carolina, home.

Perri Crutcher, for years a professional floral designer and stylist in Paris and New York City, produces elegant floral creations at Perri Ltd., his equally elegant floral decor studio in Asheville, North Carolina.

Maureen S. (Cha Cha) Donahue is a graphic artist who also makes and sells wooden and ceramic clocks. Much as she loves her five cats, she still misses her Harley.

Sheila Ennis-Shulz, one of the most fascinating artists on the East Coast, writes lyrical fiction and enjoys metaphysical spelunking when she's not doing decorative painting for Boston cosmopolites.

Katherine Graham is a published poet as well as a painter who creates wonderfully imaginative cabinets and doors on commission in Asheville, North Carolina.

Liz Hughey is a self-taught, parttime artist whose present creative passions are decorating recycled bottles at home in Gainesville, Florida, and raising the most intelligent, perceptive, and alert two year old on the planet.

Dana Irwin designs books, posters, and wonderful art of all kinds with a creative commitment that leaves onlookers gasping. She lives among her beloved Blue Ridge Mountains in western North Carolina.

Elena Lange, disguised during the day as a clinical social worker and civic activist, in her creative, real life tends her flower garden and is renovating her North Carolina home using many of the same block-printing techniques she applies to flowerpots.

Shelley Lowell owns Pink Neck Gallery, a contemporary art gallery in Asheville, North Carolina. A painter, sculptor, illustrator, graphic designer, and art teacher, she received her BFA at Pratt Institute.

Nancy McGaha creates original beadwork and needlework in Swannanoa, North Carolina.

Jean Tomaso Moore is an all-around Asheville, North Carolina, craftsperson whose talents range from potting to multimedia decoupage.

Dolly Lutz Morris is an accomplished craftsperson on too many fronts to mention. The author of *The Flower Drying Handbook* (Sterling/Lark 1996), she markets her hand-sculpted one-of-a-kind dolls, angels, and animal figures from her workshops in Saegertown, Pennsylvania.

Jean Wall Penland paints and teaches in the mountains of western North Carolina. She is the recipient of Pollock-Krasner and Adolph and Esther Gottlieb Foundation grants.

Cathy Smith is a multimedia artist whose repertoire includes woodworking, sculpture, and painting, inspired by ancient cultures and the natural world—right now the beauty around her new western North Carolina home.

Terry Taylor creates art for the garden using the pique-assiette medium, which he also combines with tramp art carving to make decorative objects for interiors. He collects, creates, and casts gentle aspersions from his charming cottage in western North Carolina.

Sharon Tompkins is a decorative painter who transforms everything from walls to flowerpots.

Pamella (Wil) Wilson is an accomplished potter and visual artist whose fine work and gentle personality have made her celebrated from the Phoenix badlands to the North Carolina highlands.

Ellen Zahorec is a mixed-media studio artist in Cincinnati, Ohio, who specializes in handmade paper and collage. Her work, shown internationally, is part of numerous private and corporate collections.

Index